BORDERS.
CLASSICS

BEOWULF

Verse Translated by
Francis Burton Gummere

Prose Translated by
Clarence Griffin Child

BORDERS.
CLASSICS

Please direct sales or editorial inquiries to:
BordersTradeBookInventoryQuestions@bordersgroupinc.com

This edition is published by
Borders Classics, an imprint of Borders Group, Inc.,
by special arrangement with
Ann Arbor Media Group, LLC
2500 South State Street, Ann Arbor, MI 48104

Printed and bound in the United States of America
by Edwards Brothers, Inc.

Quality Paperback ISBN 13: 978-1-58726-480-1
ISBN 10: 1-58726-480-3

11   10   09   08   07   10 9 8 7 6 5 4 3 2 1

CONTENTS

BEOWULF

VERSE

Prelude

Lo! praise of the prowess of people-kings
of spear-armed Danes, in days long sped,
we have heard, and what honor the athelings won!
Oft Scyld the Scefing from squadroned foes,
from many a tribe, the mead-bench tore,
awing the earls. Since erst he lay
friendless, a foundling, fate repaid him:
for he waxed under welkin, in wealth he throve,
till before him the folk, both far and near,
who house by the whale-path, heard his mandate,
gave him gifts: a good king he!
To him an heir was afterward born,
a son in his halls, whom heaven sent
to favor the folk, feeling their woe
that erst they had lacked an earl for leader
so long a while; the Lord endowed him,
the Wielder of Wonder, with world's renown.
Famed was this Beow: far flew the boast of him,
son of Scyld, in the Scandian lands.
So becomes it a youth to quit him well
with his father's friends, by fee and gift,
that to aid him, aged, in after days,
come warriors willing, should war draw nigh,
liegemen loyal: by lauded deeds
shall an earl have honor in every clan.
Forth he fared at the fated moment,
sturdy Scyld to the shelter of God.
Then they bore him over to ocean's billow,
loving clansmen, as late he charged them,
while wielded words the winsome Scyld,
the leader beloved who long had ruled.
In the roadstead rocked a ring-dight vessel,
ice-flecked, outbound, atheling's barge:

there laid they down their darling lord
on the breast of the boat, the breaker-of-rings,
by the mast the mighty one. Many a treasure
fetched from far was freighted with him.
No ship have I known so nobly dight
with weapons of war and weeds of battle,
with breastplate and blade: on his bosom lay
a heaped hoard that hence should go
far o'er the flood with him floating away.
No less these loaded the lordly gifts,
thanes' huge treasure, than those had done
who in former time forth had sent him
sole on the seas, a suckling child.
High o'er his head they hoist the standard,
a gold-wove banner; let billows take him,
gave him to ocean. Grave were their spirits,
mournful their mood. No man is able
to say in sooth, no son of the halls,
no hero 'neath heaven—who harbored that freight!

1

Now Beowulf bode in the burg of the Scyldings,
leader beloved, and long he ruled
in fame with all folk, since his father had gone
away from the world, till awoke an heir,
haughty Healfdene, who held through life,
sage and sturdy, the Scyldings glad.
Then, one after one, there woke to him,
to the chieftain of clansmen, children four:
Heorogar, then Hrothgar, then Halga brave;
and I heard that Yrse was Onela's queen,
the Heatho-Scylfing's helpmate dear.
To Hrothgar was given such glory of war,
such honor of combat, that all his kin
obeyed him gladly till great grew his band
of youthful comrades. It came in his mind

to bid his henchmen a hall uprear,
a master mead-house, mightier far
than ever was seen by the sons of earth,
and within it, then, to old and young
he would all allot that the Lord had sent him,
save only the land and the lives of his men.
Wide, I heard, was the work commanded,
for many a tribe this mid-earth round,
to fashion the folkstead. It fell, as he ordered,
in rapid achievement that ready it stood there,
of halls the noblest: Heorot he named it
whose message had might in many a land.
Not reckless of promise, the rings he dealt,
treasure at banquet: there towered the hall,
high, gabled wide, the hot surge waiting
of furious flame. Nor far was that day
when father and son-in-law stood in feud
for warfare and hatred that woke again.
With envy and anger an evil spirit
endured the dole in his dark abode,
that he heard each day the din of revel
high in the hall: there harps rang out,
clear song of the singer. He sang who knew
tales of the early time of man,
how the Almighty made the earth,
fairest fields enfolded by water,
set, triumphant, sun and moon
for a light to lighten the land-dwellers,
and braided bright the breast of earth
with limbs and leaves, made life for all
of mortal beings that breathe and move.
So lived the clansmen in cheer and revel
a winsome life, till one began
to fashion evils, that field of hell.
Grendel this monster grim was called,
march-riever mighty, in moorland living,
in fen and fastness; fief of the giants
the hapless wight a while had kept
since the Creator his exile doomed.
On kin of Cain was the killing avenged

by sovran God for slaughtered Abel.
Ill fared his feud, and far was he driven,
for the slaughter's sake, from sight of men.
Of Cain awoke all that woeful breed,
Etins and elves and evil-spirits,
as well as the giants that warred with God
weary while: but their wage was paid them!

2

Went he forth to find at fall of night
that haughty house, and heed wherever
the Ring-Danes, outrevelled, to rest had gone.
Found within it the atheling band
asleep after feasting and fearless of sorrow,
of human hardship. Unhallowed wight,
grim and greedy, he grasped betimes,
wrathful, reckless, from resting-places,
thirty of the thanes, and thence he rushed
fain of his fell spoil, faring homeward,
laden with slaughter, his lair to seek.
Then at the dawning, as day was breaking,
the might of Grendel to men was known;
then after wassail was wail uplifted,
loud moan in the morn. The mighty chief,
atheling excellent, unblithe sat,
labored in woe for the loss of his thanes,
when once had been traced the trail of the fiend,
spirit accurst: too cruel that sorrow,
too long, too loathsome. Not late the respite;
with night returning, anew began
ruthless murder; he recked no whit,
firm in his guilt, of the feud and crime.
They were easy to find who elsewhere sought
in room remote their rest at night,
bed in the bowers, when that bale was shown,
was seen in sooth, with surest token,

the hall-thane's hate. Such held themselves
far and fast who the fiend outran!
Thus ruled unrighteous and raged his fill
one against all; until empty stood
that lordly building, and long it bode so.
Twelve years' tide the trouble he bore,
sovran of Scyldings, sorrows in plenty,
boundless cares. There came unhidden
tidings true to the tribes of men,
in sorrowful songs, how ceaselessly Grendel
harassed Hrothgar, what hate he bore him,
what murder and massacre, many a year,
feud unfading, refused consent
to deal with any of Daneland's earls,
make pact of peace, or compound for gold:
still less did the wise men ween to get
great fee for the feud from his fiendish hands.
But the evil one ambushed old and young
death-shadow dark, and dogged them still,
lured, or lurked in the livelong night
of misty moorlands: men may say not
where the haunts of these Hell-Runes be.
Such heaping of horrors the hater of men,
lonely roamer, wrought unceasing,
harassings heavy. O'er Heorot he lorded,
gold-bright hall, in gloomy nights;
and ne'er could the prince approach his throne—
'twas judgment of God—or have joy in his hall.
Sore was the sorrow to Scyldings'-friend,
heart-rending misery. Many nobles
sat assembled, and searched out counsel
how it were best for bold-hearted men
against harassing terror to try their hand.
Whiles they vowed in their heathen fanes
altar-offerings, asked with words
that the slayer-of-souls would succor give them
for the pain of their people. Their practice this,
their heathen hope; 'twas Hell they thought of
in mood of their mind. Almighty they knew not,
Doomsman of Deeds and dreadful Lord,

nor Heaven's-Helmet heeded they ever,
Wielder-of-Wonder. Woe for that man
who in harm and hatred hales his soul
to fiery embraces; nor favor nor change
awaits he ever. But well for him
that after death-day may draw to his Lord,
and friendship find in the Father's arms!

3

Thus seethed unceasing the son of Healfdene
with the woe of these days; not wisest men
assuaged his sorrow; too sore the anguish,
loathly and long, that lay on his folk,
most baneful of burdens and bales of the night.
This heard in his home Hygelac's thane,
great among Geats, of Grendel's doings.
He was the mightiest man of valor
in that same day of this our life,
stalwart and stately. A stout wave-walker
he bade make ready. Yon battle-king, said he,
far o'er the swan-road he fain would seek,
the noble monarch who needed men!
The prince's journey by prudent folk
was little blamed, though they loved him dear;
they whetted the hero, and hailed good omens.
And now the bold one from bands of Geats
comrades chose, the keenest of warriors
e'er he could find; with fourteen men
the sea-wood he sought, and, sailor proved,
led them on to the land's confines.
Time had now flown; afloat was the ship,
boat under bluff. On board they climbed,
warriors ready; waves were churning
sea with sand; the sailors bore
on the breast of the bark their bright array,
their mail and weapons: the men pushed off,

on its willing way, the well-braced craft.
Then moved o'er the waters by might of the wind
that bark like a bird with breast of foam,
till in season due, on the second day,
the curved prow such course had run
that sailors now could see the land,
sea-cliffs shining, steep high hills,
headlands broad. Their haven was found,
their journey ended. Up then quickly
the Weders' clansmen climbed ashore,
anchored their sea-wood, with armor clashing
and gear of battle: God they thanked
or passing in peace o'er the paths of the sea.
Now saw from the cliff a Scylding clansman,
a warden that watched the water-side,
how they bore o'er the gangway glittering shields,
war-gear in readiness; wonder seized him
to know what manner of men they were.
Straight to the strand his steed he rode,
Hrothgar's henchman; with hand of might
he shook his spear, and spake in parley.
"Who are ye, then, ye armed men,
mailed folk, that yon mighty vessel
have urged thus over the ocean ways,
here o'er the waters? A warden I,
sentinel set o'er the sea-march here,
lest any foe to the folk of Danes
with harrying fleet should harm the land.
No aliens ever at ease thus bore them,
linden-wielders: yet word-of-leave
clearly ye lack from clansmen here,
my folk's agreement. A greater ne'er saw I
of warriors in world than is one of you,
yon hero in harness! No henchman he
worthied by weapons, if witness his features,
his peerless presence! I pray you, though, tell
your folk and home, lest hence ye fare
suspect to wander your way as spies
in Danish land. Now, dwellers afar,
ocean-travellers, take from me

simple advice: the sooner the better
I hear of the country whence ye came."

4

To him the stateliest spake in answer;
the warriors' leader his word-hoard unlocked:
"We are by kin of the clan of Geats,
and Hygelac's own hearth-fellows we.
To folk afar was my father known,
noble atheling, Ecgtheow named.
Full of winters, he fared away
aged from earth; he is honored still
through width of the world by wise men all.
To thy lord and liege in loyal mood
we hasten hither, to Healfdene's son,
people-protector: be pleased to advise us!
To that mighty-one come we on mickle errand,
to the lord of the Danes; nor deem I right
that aught be hidden. We hear—thou knowest
if sooth it is—the saying of men,
that amid the Scyldings a scathing monster,
dark ill-doer, in dusky nights
shows terrific his rage unmatched,
hatred and murder. To Hrothgar I
in greatness of soul would succor bring,
so the Wise-and-Brave may worst his foes,
if ever the end of ills is fated,
of cruel contest, if cure shall follow,
and the boiling care-waves cooler grow;
else ever afterward anguish-days
he shall suffer in sorrow while stands in place
high on its hill that house unpeered!"
Astride his steed, the strand-ward answered,
clansman unquailing: "The keen-souled thane
must be skilled to sever and sunder duly
words and works, if he well intends.

I gather, this band is graciously bent
to the Scyldings' master. March, then, bearing
weapons and weeds the way I show you.
I will bid my men your boat meanwhile
to guard for fear lest foemen come,
your new-tarred ship by shore of ocean
faithfully watching till once again
it waft o'er the waters those well-loved thanes—
winding-neck'd wood—to Weders' bounds,
heroes such as the hest of fate
shall succor and save from the shock of war."
They bent them to march, the boat lay still,
fettered by cable and fast at anchor,
broad-bosomed ship. Then shone the boars
over the cheek-guard; chased with gold,
keen and gleaming, guard it kept
o'er the man of war, as marched along
heroes in haste, till the hall they saw,
broad of gable and bright with gold:
that was the fairest, 'mid folk of earth,
of houses 'neath heaven, where Hrothgar lived,
and the gleam of it lightened o'er lands afar.
The sturdy shieldsman showed that bright
burg-of-the-boldest; bade them go
straightway thither; his steed then turned,
hardy hero, and hailed them thus:
"'Tis time that I fare from you. Father Almighty
in grace and mercy guard you well,
safe in your seekings. Seaward I go,
'gainst hostile warriors hold my watch."

5

Stone-bright the street: it showed the way
to the crowd of clansmen. Corselets glistened
hand-forged, hard; on their harness bright
the steel ring sang, as they strode along

in mail of battle, and marched to the hall.
There, weary of ocean, the wall along
they set their bucklers, their broad shields, down,
and bowed them to bench: the breastplates clanged,
war-gear of men; their weapons stacked,
spears of the seafarers stood together,
gray-tipped ash: that iron band
was worthily weaponed! A warrior proud
asked of the heroes their home and kin.
"Whence, now, bear ye burnished shields,
harness gray and helmets grim,
spears in multitude? Messenger, I,
Hrothgar's herald! Heroes so many
ne'er met I as strangers of mood so strong.
'Tis plain that for prowess, not plunged into exile,
for high-hearted valor, Hrothgar ye seek!"
Him the sturdy-in-war bespake with words,
proud earl of the Weders answer made,
hardy 'neath helmet: "Hygelac's, we,
fellows at board; I am Beowulf named.
I am seeking to say to the son of Healfdene
this mission of mine, to thy master-lord,
the doughty prince, if he deign at all
grace that we greet him, the good one, now."
Wulfgar spake, the Wendles' chieftain,
whose might of mind to many was known,
his courage and counsel: "The king of Danes,
the Scyldings' friend, I fain will tell,
the Breaker-of-Rings, as the boon thou askest,
the famed prince, of thy faring hither,
and, swiftly after, such answer bring
as the doughty monarch may deign to give."
Hied then in haste to where Hrothgar sat
white-haired and old, his earls about him,
till the stout thane stood at the shoulder there
of the Danish king: good courtier he!
Wulfgar spake to his winsome lord:
"Hither have fared to thee far-come men
o'er the paths of ocean, people of Geatland;
and the stateliest there by his sturdy band

is Beowulf named. This boon they seek,
that they, my master, may with thee
have speech at will: nor spurn their prayer
to give them hearing, gracious Hrothgar!
In weeds of the warrior worthy they,
methinks, of our liking; their leader most surely,
a hero that hither his henchmen has led."

6

Hrothgar answered, helmet of Scyldings:
"I knew him of yore in his youthful days;
his aged father was Ecgtheow named,
to whom, at home, gave Hrethel the Geat
his only daughter. Their offspring bold
fares hither to seek the steadfast friend.
And seamen, too, have said me this—
who carried my gifts to the Geatish court,
thither for thanks—he has thirty men's
heft of grasp in the gripe of his hand,
the bold-in-battle. Blessed God
out of his mercy this man hath sent
to Danes of the West, as I ween indeed,
against horror of Grendel. I hope to give
the good youth gold for his gallant thought.
Be thou in haste, and bid them hither,
clan of kinsmen, to come before me;
and add this word, they are welcome guests
to folk of the Danes."
[To the door of the hall
Wulfgar went] and the word declared:
"To you this message my master sends,
East-Danes' king, that your kin he knows,
hardy heroes, and hails you all
welcome hither o'er waves of the sea!
Ye may wend your way in war-attire,
and under helmets Hrothgar greet;

but let here the battle-shields bide your parley,
and wooden war-shafts wait its end."
Uprose the mighty one, ringed with his men,
brave band of thanes: some bode without,
battle-gear guarding, as bade the chief.
Then hied that troop where the herald led them,
under Heorot's roof [the hero strode,]
hardy 'neath helm, till the hearth he neared.
Beowulf spake, his breastplate gleamed,
war-net woven by wit of the smith:
"Thou Hrothgar, hail! Hygelac's I,
kinsman and follower. Fame a plenty
have I gained in youth! These Grendel deeds
I heard in my homeland heralded clear.
Seafarers say how stands this hall,
of buildings best, for your band of thanes
empty and idle, when evening sun
in the harbor of heaven is hidden away.
So my vassals advised me well,
brave and wise, the best of men,
O sovran Hrothgar, to seek thee here,
for my nerve and my might they knew full well.
Themselves had seen me from slaughter come
blood-flecked from foes, where five I bound,
and that wild brood worsted. I' the waves I slew
nicors by night, in need and peril
avenging the Weders, whose woe they sought,
crushing the grim ones. Grendel now,
monster cruel, be mine to quell
in single battle! So, from thee,
thou sovran of the Shining-Danes,
Scyldings'-bulwark, a boon I seek,
and, Friend-of-the-folk, refuse it not,
O Warriors'-shield, now I've wandered far,
that I alone with my liegemen here,
this hardy band, may Heorot purge!
More I hear, that the monster dire,
in his wanton mood, of weapons recks not;
hence shall I scorn—so Hygelac stay,
king of my kindred, kind to me!—

brand or buckler to bear in the fight,
gold-colored targe: but with gripe alone
must I front the fiend and fight for life,
foe against foe. Then faith be his
in the doom of the Lord whom death shall take.
Fain, I ween, if the fight he win,
in this hall of gold my Geatish band
will he fearless eat—as oft before—
my noblest thanes. Nor need'st thou then
to hide my head; for his shall I be,
dyed in gore, if death must take me;
and my blood-covered body he'll bear as prey,
ruthless devour it, the roamer-lonely,
with my life-blood redden his lair in the fen:
no further for me need'st food prepare!
To Hygelac send, if Hild should take me,
best of war-weeds, warding my breast,
armor excellent, heirloom of Hrethel
and work of Wayland. Fares Wyrd as she must."

7

Hrothgar spake, the Scyldings'-helmet:
"For fight defensive, Friend my Beowulf,
to succor and save, thou hast sought us here.
Thy father's combat a feud enkindled
when Heatholaf with hand he slew
among the Wylfings; his Weder kin
for horror of fighting feared to hold him.
Fleeing, he sought our South-Dane folk,
over surge of ocean the Honor-Scyldings,
when first I was ruling the folk of Danes,
wielded, youthful, this widespread realm,
this hoard-hold of heroes. Heorogar was dead,
my elder brother, had breathed his last,
Healfdene's bairn: he was better than I!
Straightway the feud with fee I settled,

to the Wylfings sent, o'er watery ridges,
treasures olden: oaths he swore me.
Sore is my soul to say to any
of the race of man what ruth for me
in Heorot Grendel with hate hath wrought,
what sudden harryings. Hall-folk fail me,
my warriors wane; for Wyrd hath swept them
into Grendel's grasp. But God is able
this deadly foe from his deeds to turn!
Boasted full oft, as my beer they drank,
earls o'er the ale-cup, armed men,
that they would bide in the beer-hall here,
Grendel's attack with terror of blades.
Then was this mead-house at morning tide
dyed with gore, when the daylight broke,
all the boards of the benches blood-besprinkled,
gory the hall: I had heroes the less,
doughty dear-ones that death had reft.
But sit to the banquet, unbind thy words,
hardy hero, as heart shall prompt thee."

Gathered together, the Geatish men
in the banquet-hall on bench assigned,
sturdy-spirited, sat them down,
hardy-hearted. A henchman attended,
carried the carven cup in hand,
served the clear mead. Oft minstrels sang
blithe in Heorot. Heroes revelled,
no dearth of warriors, Weder and Dane.

8

Unferth spake, the son of Ecglaf,
who sat at the feet of the Scyldings' lord,
unbound the battle-runes. Beowulf's quest,
sturdy seafarer's, sorely galled him;
ever he envied that other men

should more achieve in middle-earth
of fame under heaven than he himself.
"Art thou that Beowulf, Breca's rival,
who emulous swam on the open sea,
when for pride the pair of you proved the floods,
and wantonly dared in waters deep
to risk your lives? No living man,
or lief or loath, from your labor dire
could you dissuade, from swimming the main.
Ocean-tides with your arms ye covered,
with strenuous hands the sea-streets measured,
swam o'er the waters. Winter's storm
rolled the rough waves. In realm of sea
a sennight strove ye. In swimming he topped thee,
had more of main! Him at morning-tide
billows bore to the Battling Reamas,
whence he hied to his home so dear
beloved of his liegemen, to land of Brondings,
fastness fair, where his folk he ruled,
town and treasure. In triumph o'er thee
Beanstan's bairn his boast achieved.
So ween I for thee a worse adventure—
though in buffet of battle thou brave hast been,
in struggle grim—if Grendel's approach
thou darst await through the watch of night!"

Beowulf spake, bairn of Ecgtheow:
"What a deal hast uttered, dear my Unferth,
drunken with beer, of Breca now,
told of his triumph! Truth I claim it,
that I had more of might in the sea
than any man else, more ocean-endurance.
We twain had talked, in time of youth,
and made our boast—we were merely boys,
striplings still—to stake our lives
far at sea: and so we performed it.
Naked swords, as we swam along,
we held in hand, with hope to guard us
against the whales. Not a whit from me

could he float afar o'er the flood of waves,
haste o'er the billows; nor him I abandoned.
Together we twain on the tides abode
five nights full till the flood divided us,
churning waves and chillest weather,
darkling night, and the northern wind
ruthless rushed on us: rough was the surge.
Now the wrath of the sea-fish rose apace;
yet me 'gainst the monsters my mailed coat,
hard and hand-linked, help afforded,
battle-sark braided my breast to ward,
garnished with gold. There grasped me firm
and haled me to bottom the hated foe,
with grimmest gripe. 'Twas granted me, though,
to pierce the monster with point of sword,
with blade of battle: huge beast of the sea
was whelmed by the hurly through hand of mine."

9

"Me thus often the evil monsters
thronging threatened. With thrust of my sword,
the darling, I dealt them due return!
Nowise had they bliss from their booty then
to devour their victim, vengeful creatures,
seated to banquet at bottom of sea;
but at break of day, by my brand sore hurt,
on the edge of ocean up they lay,
put to sleep by the sword. And since, by them
on the fathomless sea-ways sailor-folk
are never molested. Light from east,
came bright God's beacon; the billows sank,
so that I saw the sea-cliffs high,
windy walls. For Wyrd oft saveth
earl undoomed if he doughty be!
And so it came that I killed with my sword
nine of the nicors. Of night-fought battles

ne'er heard I a harder 'neath heaven's dome,
nor adrift on the deep a more desolate man!
Yet I came unharmed from that hostile clutch,
though spent with swimming. The sea upbore me,
flood of the tide, on Finnish land,
the welling waters. No wise of thee
have I heard men tell such terror of falchions,
bitter battle. Breca ne'er yet,
not one of you pair, in the play of war
such daring deed has done at all
with bloody brand—I boast not of it!—
though thou wast the bane of thy brethren dear,
thy closest kin, whence curse of hell
awaits thee, well as thy wit may serve!
For I say in sooth, thou son of Ecglaf,
never had Grendel these grim deeds wrought,
monster dire, on thy master dear,
in Heorot such havoc, if heart of thine
were as battle-bold as thy boast is loud!
But he has found no feud will happen;
from sword-clash dread of your Danish clan
he vaunts him safe, from the Victor-Scyldings.
He forces pledges, favors none
of the land of Danes, but lustily murders,
fights and feasts, nor feud he dreads
from Spear-Dane men. But speedily now
shall I prove him the prowess and pride of the Geats,
shall bid him battle. Blithe to mead
go he that listeth, when light of dawn
this morrow morning o'er men of earth,
ether-robed sun from the south shall beam!"
Joyous then was the Jewel-giver,
hoar-haired, war-brave; help awaited
the Bright-Danes' prince, from Beowulf hearing,
folk's good shepherd, such firm resolve.
Then was laughter of liegemen loud resounding
with winsome words. Came Wealhtheow forth,
queen of Hrothgar, heedful of courtesy,
gold-decked, greeting the guests in hall;
and the high-born lady handed the cup

first to the East-Danes' heir and warden,
bade him be blithe at the beer-carouse,
the land's beloved one. Lustily took he
banquet and beaker, battle-famed king.

Through the hall then went the Helmings' Lady,
to younger and older everywhere
carried the cup, till come the moment
when the ring-graced queen, the royal-hearted,
to Beowulf bore the beaker of mead.
She greeted the Geats' lord, God she thanked,
in wisdom's words, that her will was granted,
that at last on a hero her hope could lean
for comfort in terrors. The cup he took,
hardy-in-war, from Wealhtheow's hand,
and answer uttered the eager-for-combat.
Beowulf spake, bairn of Ecgtheow:
"This was my thought, when my thanes and I
bent to the ocean and entered our boat,
that I would work the will of your people
fully, or fighting fall in death,
in fiend's gripe fast. I am firm to do
an earl's brave deed, or end the days
of this life of mine in the mead-hall here."
Well these words to the woman seemed,
Beowulf's battle-boast. Bright with gold
the stately dame by her spouse sat down.
Again, as erst, began in hall
warriors' wassail and words of power,
the proud-band's revel, till presently
the son of Healfdene hastened to seek
rest for the night; he knew there waited
fight for the fiend in that festal hall,
when the sheen of the sun they saw no more,
and dusk of night sank darkling nigh,
and shadowy shapes came striding on,
wan under welkin. The warriors rose.
Man to man, he made harangue,
Hrothgar to Beowulf, bade him hail,
let him wield the wine hall: a word he added:

"Never to any man erst I trusted,
since I could heave up hand and shield,
this noble Dane-Hall, till now to thee.
Have now and hold this house unpeered;
remember thy glory; thy might declare;
watch for the foe! No wish shall fail thee
if thou bidest the battle with bold-won life."

10

Then Hrothgar went with his hero-train,
defence-of-Scyldings, forth from hall;
fain would the war-lord Wealhtheow seek,
couch of his queen. The King-of-Glory
against this Grendel a guard had set,
so heroes heard, a hall-defender,
who warded the monarch and watched for the monster.
In truth, the Geats' prince gladly trusted
his mettle, his might, the mercy of God!
Cast off then his corselet of iron,
helmet from head; to his henchman gave,
choicest of weapons, the well-chased sword,
bidding him guard the gear of battle.
Spake then his Vaunt the valiant man,
Beowulf Geat, ere the bed be sought:
"Of force in fight no feebler I count me,
in grim war-deeds, than Grendel deems him.
Not with the sword, then, to sleep of death
his life will I give, though it lie in my power.
No skill is his to strike against me,
my shield to hew though he hardy be,
bold in battle; we both, this night,
shall spurn the sword, if he seek me here,
unweaponed, for war. Let wisest God,
sacred Lord, on which side soever
doom decree as he deemeth right."
Reclined then the chieftain, and cheek-pillows held

the head of the earl, while all about him
seamen hardy on hall-beds sank.
None of them thought that thence their steps
to the folk and fastness that fostered them,
to the land they loved, would lead them back!
Full well they wist that on warriors many
battle-death seized, in the banquet-hall,
of Danish clan. But comfort and help,
war-weal weaving, to Weder folk
the Master gave, that, by might of one,
over their enemy all prevailed,
by single strength. In sooth 'tis told
that highest God o'er human kind
hath wielded ever! Thro' wan night striding,
came the walker-in-shadow. Warriors slept
whose hest was to guard the gabled hall,
all save one. 'Twas widely known
that against God's will the ghostly ravager
him could not hurl to haunts of darkness;
wakeful, ready, with warrior's wrath,
bold he bided the battle's issue.

11

Then from the moorland, by misty crags,
with God's wrath laden, Grendel came.
The monster was minded of mankind now
sundry to seize in the stately house.
Under welkin he walked, till the wine-palace there,
gold-hall of men, he gladly discerned,
flashing with fretwork. Not first time, this,
that he the home of Hrothgar sought,
yet ne'er in his life-day, late or early,
such hardy heroes, such hall-thanes, found!
To the house the warrior walked apace,
parted from peace; the portal opened,

though with forged bolts fast, when his fists had struck it,
and baleful he burst in his blatant rage,
the house's mouth. All hastily, then,
o'er fair-paved floor the fiend trod on,
ireful he strode; there streamed from his eyes
fearful flashes, like flame to see.

He spied in hall the hero-band,
kin and clansmen clustered asleep,
hardy liegemen. Then laughed his heart;
for the monster was minded, ere morn should dawn,
savage, to sever the soul of each,
life from body, since lusty banquet
waited his will! But Wyrd forbade him
to seize any more of men on earth
after that evening. Eagerly watched
Hygelac's kinsman his cursed foe,
how he would fare in fell attack.
Not that the monster was minded to pause!
Straightway he seized a sleeping warrior
for the first, and tore him fiercely asunder,
the bone-frame bit, drank blood in streams,
swallowed him piecemeal: swiftly thus
the lifeless corpse was clear devoured,
e'en feet and hands. Then farther he hied;
for the hardy hero with hand he grasped,
felt for the foe with fiendish claw,
for the hero reclining, who clutched it boldly,
prompt to answer, propped on his arm.
Soon then saw that shepherd-of-evils
that never he met in this middle-world,
in the ways of earth, another wight
with heavier hand-gripe; at heart he feared,
sorrowed in soul, none the sooner escaped!
Fain would he flee, his fastness seek,
the den of devils: no doings now
such as oft he had done in days of old!
Then bethought him the hardy Hygelac-thane
of his boast at evening: up he bounded,

grasped firm his foe, whose fingers cracked.
The fiend made off, but the earl close followed.
The monster meant—if he might at all—
to fling himself free, and far away
fly to the fens, knew his fingers' power
in the gripe of the grim one. Gruesome march
to Heorot this monster of harm had made!
Din filled the room; the Danes were bereft,
castle-dwellers and clansmen all,
earls, of their ale. Angry were both
those savage hall-guards: the house resounded.
Wonder it was the wine-hall firm
in the strain of their struggle stood, to earth
the fair house fell not; too fast it was
within and without by its iron bands
craftily clamped; though there crashed from sill
many a mead-bench—men have told me—
gay with gold, where the grim foes wrestled.
So well had weened the wisest Scyldings
that not ever at all might any man
that bone-decked, brave house break asunder,
crush by craft, unless clasp of fire
in smoke engulfed it. Again uprose
din redoubled. Danes of the North
with fear and frenzy were filled, each one,
who from the wall that wailing heard,
God's foe sounding his grisly song,
cry of the conquered, clamorous pain
from captive of hell. Too closely held him
he who of men in might was strongest
in that same day of this our life.

12

Not in any wise would the earls'-defence
suffer that slaughterous stranger to live,

useless deeming his days and years
to men on earth. Now many an earl
of Beowulf brandished blade ancestral,
fain the life of their lord to shield,
their praised prince, if power were theirs;
never they knew—as they neared the foe,
hardy-hearted heroes of war,
aiming their swords on every side
the accursed to kill—no keenest blade,
no farest of falchions fashioned on earth,
could harm or hurt that hideous fiend!
He was safe, by his spells, from sword of battle,
from edge of iron. Yet his end and parting
on that same day of this our life
woeful should be, and his wandering soul
far off flit to the fiends' domain.
Soon he found, who in former days,
harmful in heart and hated of God,
on many a man such murder wrought,
that the frame of his body failed him now.
For him the keen-souled kinsman of Hygelac
held in hand; hateful alive
was each to other. The outlaw dire
took mortal hurt; a mighty wound
showed on his shoulder, and sinews cracked,
and the bone-frame burst. To Beowulf now
the glory was given, and Grendel thence
death-sick his den in the dark moor sought,
noisome abode: he knew too well
that here was the last of life, an end
of his days on earth. To all the Danes
by that bloody battle the boon had come.
From ravage had rescued the roving stranger
Hrothgar's hall; the hardy and wise one
had purged it anew. His night-work pleased him,
his deed and its honor. To Eastern Danes
had the valiant Geat his vaunt made good,
all their sorrow and ills assuaged,
their bale of battle borne so long,

and all the dole they erst endured
pain a-plenty. 'Twas proof of this,
when the hardy-in-fight a hand laid down,
arm and shoulder—all, indeed,
of Grendel's gripe—'neath the gabled roof.

13

Many at morning, as men have told me,
warriors gathered the gift-hall round,
folk-leaders faring from far and near,
o'er wide-stretched ways, the wonder to view,
trace of the traitor. Not troublous seemed
the enemy's end to any man
who saw by the gait of the graceless foe
how the weary-hearted, away from thence,
baffled in battle and banned, his steps
death-marked dragged to the devils' mere.
Bloody the billows were boiling there,
turbid the tide of tumbling waves
horribly seething, with sword-blood hot,
by that doomed one dyed, who in den of the moor
laid forlorn his life adown,
his heathen soul, and hell received it.
Home then rode the hoary clansmen
from that merry journey, and many a youth,
on horses white, the hardy warriors,
back from the mere. Then Beowulf's glory
eager they echoed, and all averred
that from sea to sea, or south or north,
there was no other in earth's domain,
under vault of heaven, more valiant found,
of warriors none more worthy to rule!
(On their lord beloved they laid no slight,
gracious Hrothgar: a good king he!)
From time to time, the tried-in-battle

their gray steeds set to gallop amain,
and ran a race when the road seemed fair.
From time to time, a thane of the king,
who had made many vaunts, and was mindful of verses,
stored with sagas and songs of old,
bound word to word in well-knit rime,
welded his lay; this warrior soon
of Beowulf's quest right cleverly sang,
and artfully added an excellent tale,
in well-ranged words, of the warlike deeds
he had heard in saga of Sigemund.
Strange the story: he said it all,
the Waelsing's wanderings wide, his struggles,
which never were told to tribes of men,
the feuds and the frauds, save to Fitela only,
when of these doings he deigned to speak,
uncle to nephew; as ever the twain
stood side by side in stress of war,
and multitude of the monster kind
they had felled with their swords. Of Sigemund grew,
when he passed from life, no little praise;
for the doughty-in-combat a dragon killed
that herded the hoard: under hoary rock
the atheling dared the deed alone
fearful quest, nor was Fitela there.
Yet so it befell, his falchion pierced
that wondrous worm—on the wall it struck,
best blade; the dragon died in its blood.
Thus had the dread-one by daring achieved
over the ring-hoard to rule at will,
himself to pleasure; a sea-boat he loaded,
and bore on its bosom the beaming gold,
son of Waels; the worm was consumed.
He had of all heroes the highest renown
among races of men, this refuge-of-warriors,
for deeds of daring that decked his name
since the hand and heart of Heremod
grew slack in battle. He, swiftly banished
to mingle with monsters at mercy of foes,

to death was betrayed; for torrents of sorrow
had lamed him too long; a load of care
to earls and athelings all he proved.
Oft indeed, in earlier days,
for the warrior's wayfaring wise men mourned,
who had hoped of him help from harm and bale,
and had thought their sovran's son would thrive,
follow his father, his folk protect,
the hoard and the stronghold, heroes' land,
home of Scyldings. But here, thanes said,
the kinsman of Hygelac kinder seemed
to all: the other was urged to crime!
And afresh to the race, the fallow roads
by swift steeds measured! The morning sun
was climbing higher. Clansmen hastened
to the high-built hall, those hardy-minded,
the wonder to witness. Warden of treasure,
crowned with glory, the king himself,
with stately band from the bride-bower strode;
and with him the queen and her crowd of maidens
measured the path to the mead-house fair.

14

Hrothgar spake—to the hall he went,
stood by the steps, the steep roof saw,
garnished with gold, and Grendel's hand—
"For the sight I see to the Sovran Ruler
be speedy thanks! A throng of sorrows
I have borne from Grendel; but God still works
wonder on wonder, the Warden-of-Glory.
It was but now that I never more
for woes that weighed on me waited help
long as I lived, when, laved in blood,
stood sword-gore-stained this stateliest house,
widespread woe for wise men all,

who had no hope to hinder ever
foes infernal and fiendish sprites
from havoc in hall. This hero now,
by the Wielder's might, a work has done
that not all of us erst could ever do
by wile and wisdom. Lo, well can she say
whoso of women this warrior bore
among sons of men, if still she liveth,
that the God of the ages was good to her
in the birth of her bairn. Now, Beowulf, thee,
of heroes best, I shall heartily love
as mine own, my son; preserve thou ever
this kinship new: thou shalt never lack
wealth of the world that I wield as mine!
Full oft for less have I largess showered,
my precious hoard, on a punier man,
less stout in struggle. Thyself hast now
fulfilled such deeds, that thy fame shall endure
through all the ages. As ever he did,
well may the Wielder reward thee still!"
Beowulf spake, bairn of Ecgtheow:
"This work of war most willingly
we have fought, this fight, and fearlessly dared
force of the foe. Fain, too, were I
hadst thou but seen himself, what time
the fiend in his trappings tottered to fall!
Swiftly, I thought, in strongest gripe
on his bed of death to bind him down,
that he in the hent of this hand of mine
should breathe his last: but he broke away.
Him I might not—the Maker willed not—
hinder from flight, and firm enough hold
the life-destroyer: too sturdy was he,
the ruthless, in running! For rescue, however,
he left behind him his hand in pledge,
arm and shoulder; nor aught of help
could the cursed one thus procure at all.
None the longer liveth he, loathsome fiend,
sunk in his sins, but sorrow holds him

tightly grasped in gripe of anguish,
in baleful bonds, where bide he must,
evil outlaw, such awful doom
as the Mighty Maker shall mete him out."

More silent seemed the son of Ecglaf
in boastful speech of his battle-deeds,
since athelings all, through the earl's great prowess,
beheld that hand, on the high roof gazing,
foeman's fingers—the forepart of each
of the sturdy nails to steel was likest—
heathen's "hand-spear," hostile warrior's
claw uncanny. 'Twas clear, they said,
that him no blade of the brave could touch,
how keen soever, or cut away
that battle-hand bloody from baneful foe.

15

There was hurry and hest in Heorot now
for hands to bedeck it, and dense was the throng
of men and women the wine-hall to cleanse,
the guest-room to garnish. Gold-gay shone the hangings
that were wove on the wall, and wonders many
to delight each mortal that looks upon them.
Though braced within by iron bands,
that building bright was broken sorely;
rent were its hinges; the roof alone
held safe and sound, when, seared with crime,
the fiendish foe his flight essayed,
of life despairing. No light thing that,
the flight for safety, essay it who will!
Forced of fate, he shall find his way
to the refuge ready for race of man,
for soul-possessors, and sons of earth;
and there his body on bed of death

shall rest after revel. Arrived was the hour
when to hall proceeded Healfdene's son:
the king himself would sit to banquet.
Ne'er heard I of host in haughtier throng
more graciously gathered round giver-of-rings!
Bowed then to bench those bearers-of-glory,
fain of the feasting. Featly received
many a mead-cup the mighty-in-spirit,
kinsmen who sat in the sumptuous hall,
Hrothgar and Hrothulf. Heorot now
was filled with friends; the folk of Scyldings
ne'er yet had tried the traitor's deed.
To Beowulf gave the bairn of Healfdene
a gold-wove banner, guerdon of triumph,
broidered battle-flag, breastplate and helmet;
and a splendid sword was seen of many
borne to the brave one. Beowulf took
cup in hall: for such costly gifts
he suffered no shame in that soldier throng.
For I heard of few heroes, in heartier mood,
with four such gifts, so fashioned with gold,
on the ale-bench honoring others thus!
O'er the roof of the helmet high, a ridge,
wound with wires, kept ward o'er the head,
lest the relict-of-files should fierce invade,
sharp in the strife, when that shielded hero
should go to grapple against his foes.
Then the earls'-defence on the floor bade lead
coursers eight, with carven head-gear,
adown the hall: one horse was decked
with a saddle all shining and set in jewels;
'twas the battle-seat of the best of kings,
when to play of swords the son of Healfdene
was fain to fare. Ne'er failed his valor
in the crush of combat when corpses fell.
To Beowulf over them both then gave
the refuge-of-Ingwines right and power,
o'er war-steeds and weapons: wished him joy of them.
Manfully thus the mighty prince,

hoard-guard for heroes, that hard fight repaid
with steeds and treasures contemned by none
who is willing to say the sooth aright.

16

And the lord of earls, to each that came
with Beowulf over the briny ways,
an heirloom there at the ale-bench gave,
precious gift; and the price bade pay
in gold for him whom Grendel erst
murdered—and fain of them more had killed,
had not wisest God their Wyrd averted,
and the man's brave mood. The Maker then
ruled human kind, as here and now.
Therefore is insight always best,
and forethought of mind. How much awaits him
of lief and of loath, who long time here,
through days of warfare this world endures!

Then song and music mingled sounds
in the presence of Healfdene's head-of-armies
and harping was heard with the hero-lay
as Hrothgar's singer the hall-joy woke
along the mead-seats, making his song
of that sudden raid on the sons of Finn.
Healfdene's hero, Hnaef the Scylding,
was fated to fall in the Frisian slaughter.
Hildeburh needed not hold in value
her enemies' honor! Innocent both
were the loved ones she lost at the linden-play,
bairn and brother, they bowed to fate,
stricken by spears; 'twas a sorrowful woman!
None doubted why the daughter of Hoc
bewailed her doom when dawning came,
and under the sky she saw them lying,
kinsmen murdered, where most she had kenned

of the sweets of the world! By war were swept, too,
Finn's own liegemen, and few were left;
in the parleying-place he could ply no longer
weapon, nor war could he wage on Hengest,
and rescue his remnant by right of arms
from the prince's thane. A pact he offered:
another dwelling the Danes should have,
hall and high-seat, and half the power
should fall to them in Frisian land;
and at the fee-gifts, Folcwald's son
day by day the Danes should honor,
the folk of Hengest favor with rings,
even as truly, with treasure and jewels,
with fretted gold, as his Frisian kin
he meant to honor in ale-hall there.
Pact of peace they plighted further
on both sides firmly. Finn to Hengest
with oath, upon honor, openly promised
that woeful remnant, with wise-men's aid,
nobly to govern, so none of the guests
by word or work should warp the treaty,
or with malice of mind bemoan themselves
as forced to follow their fee-giver's slayer,
lordless men, as their lot ordained.
Should Frisian, moreover, with foeman's taunt,
that murderous hatred to mind recall,
then edge of the sword must seal his doom.

Oaths were given, and ancient gold
heaped from hoard. The hardy Scylding,
battle-thane best, on his balefire lay.
All on the pyre were plain to see
the gory sark, the gilded swine-crest,
boar of hard iron, and athelings many
slain by the sword: at the slaughter they fell.
It was Hildeburh's hest, at Hnaef's own pyre
the bairn of her body on brands to lay,
his bones to burn, on the balefire placed,
at his uncle's side. In sorrowful dirges
bewept them the woman: great wailing ascended.

Then wound up to welkin the wildest of death-fires,
roared o'er the hillock: heads all were melted,
gashes burst, and blood gushed out
from bites of the body. Balefire devoured,
greediest spirit, those spared not by war
out of either folk: their flower was gone.

17

Then hastened those heroes their home to see,
friendless, to find the Frisian land,
houses and high burg. Hengest still
through the death-dyed winter dwelt with Finn,
holding pact, yet of home he minded,
though powerless his ring-decked prow to drive
over the waters, now waves rolled fierce
lashed by the winds, or winter locked them
in icy fetters. Then fared another
year to men's dwellings, as yet they do,
the sunbright skies, that their season ever
duly await. Far off winter was driven;
fair lay earth's breast; and fain was the rover,
the guest, to depart, though more gladly he pondered
on wreaking his vengeance than roaming the deep,
and how to hasten the hot encounter
where sons of the Frisians were sure to be.
So he escaped not the common doom,
when Hun with "Lafing," the light-of-battle,
best of blades, his bosom pierced:
its edge was famed with the Frisian earls.
On fierce-heart Finn there fell likewise,
on himself at home, the horrid sword-death;
for Guthlaf and Oslaf of grim attack
had sorrowing told, from sea-ways landed,
mourning their woes. Finn's wavering spirit
bode not in breast. The burg was reddened
with blood of foemen, and Finn was slain,

king amid clansmen; the queen was taken.
To their ship the Scylding warriors bore
all the chattels the chieftain owned,
whatever they found in Finn's domain
of gems and jewels. The gentle wife
o'er paths of the deep to the Danes they bore,
led to her land. The lay was finished,
the gleeman's song. Then glad rose the revel;
bench-joy brightened. Bearers draw
from their "wonder-vats" wine. Comes Wealhtheow forth,
under gold-crown goes where the good pair sit,
uncle and nephew, true each to the other one,
kindred in amity. Unferth the spokesman
at the Scylding lord's feet sat: men had faith in his spirit,
his keenness of courage, though kinsmen had found him
unsure at the sword-play. The Scylding queen spoke:
"Quaff of this cup, my king and lord,
breaker of rings, and blithe be thou,
gold-friend of men; to the Geats here speak
such words of mildness as man should use.
Be glad with thy Geats; of those gifts be mindful,
or near or far, which now thou hast.

Men say to me, as son thou wishest
yon hero to hold. Thy Heorot purged,
jewel-hall brightest, enjoy while thou canst,
with many a largess; and leave to thy kin
folk and realm when forth thou goest
to greet thy doom. For gracious I deem
my Hrothulf, willing to hold and rule
nobly our youths, if thou yield up first,
prince of Scyldings, thy part in the world.
I ween with good he will well requite
offspring of ours, when all he minds
that for him we did in his helpless days
of gift and grace to gain him honor!"
Then she turned to the seat where her sons were placed,
Hrethric and Hrothmund, with heroes' bairns,
young men together: the Geat, too, sat there,
Beowulf brave, the brothers between.

18

A cup she gave him, with kindly greeting
and winsome words. Of wounden gold,
she offered, to honor him, arm-jewels twain,
corselet and rings, and of collars the noblest
that ever I knew the earth around.
Ne'er heard I so mighty, 'neath heaven's dome,
a hoard-gem of heroes, since Hama bore
to his bright-built burg the Brisings' necklace,
jewel and gem casket. Jealousy fled he,
Eormenric's hate: chose help eternal.
Hygelac Geat, grandson of Swerting,
on the last of his raids this ring bore with him,
under his banner the booty defending,
the war-spoil warding; but Wyrd o'erwhelmed him
what time, in his daring, dangers he sought,
feud with Frisians. Fairest of gems
he bore with him over the beaker-of-waves,
sovran strong: under shield he died.
Fell the corpse of the king into keeping of Franks,
gear of the breast, and that gorgeous ring;
weaker warriors won the spoil,
after gripe of battle, from Geatland's lord,
and held the death-field. Din rose in hall.
Wealhtheow spake amid warriors, and said:
"This jewel enjoy in thy jocund youth,
Beowulf lov'd, these battle-weeds wear,
a royal treasure, and richly thrive!
Preserve thy strength, and these striplings here
counsel in kindness: requital be mine.
Hast done such deeds, that for days to come
thou art famed among folk both far and near,
so wide as washeth the wave of Ocean
his windy walls. Through the ways of life
prosper, O prince! I pray for thee
rich possessions. To son of mine
be helpful in deed and uphold his joys!
Here every earl to the other is true,

mild of mood, to the master loyal!
Thanes are friendly, the throng obedient,
liegemen are revelling: list and obey!"
Went then to her place. That was proudest of feasts;
flowed wine for the warriors. Wyrd they knew not,
destiny dire, and the doom to be seen
by many an earl when eve should come,
and Hrothgar homeward hasten away,
royal, to rest. The room was guarded
by an army of earls, as erst was done.
They bared the bench-boards; abroad they spread
beds and bolsters. One beer-carouser
in danger of doom lay down in the hall.
At their heads they set their shields of war,
bucklers bright; on the bench were there
over each atheling, easy to see,
the high battle-helmet, the haughty spear,
the corselet of rings. 'Twas their custom so
ever to be for battle prepared,
at home, or harrying, which it were,
even as oft as evil threatened
their sovran king. They were clansmen good.

19

Then sank they to sleep. With sorrow one bought
his rest of the evening, as ofttime had happened
when Grendel guarded that golden hall,
evil wrought, till his end drew nigh,
slaughter for sins. 'Twas seen and told
how an avenger survived the fiend,
as was learned afar. The livelong time
after that grim fight, Grendel's mother,
monster of women, mourned her woe.
She was doomed to dwell in the dreary waters,
cold sea-courses, since Cain cut down
with edge of the sword his only brother,

his father's offspring: outlawed he fled,
marked with murder, from men's delights
warded the wilds. There woke from him
such fate-sent ghosts as Grendel, who,
war-wolf horrid, at Heorot found
a warrior watching and waiting the fray,
with whom the grisly one grappled amain.
But the man remembered his mighty power,
the glorious gift that God had sent him,
in his Maker's mercy put his trust
for comfort and help: so he conquered the foe,
felled the fiend, who fled abject,
reft of joy, to the realms of death,
mankind's foe. And his mother now,
gloomy and grim, would go that quest
of sorrow, the death of her son to avenge.
To Heorot came she, where helmeted Danes
slept in the hall. Too soon came back
old ills of the earls, when in she burst,
the mother of Grendel. Less grim, though, that terror,
e'en as terror of woman in war is less,
might of maid, than of men in arms
when, hammer-forged, the falchion hard,
sword gore-stained, through swine of the helm,
crested, with keen blade carves amain.
Then was in hall the hard-edge drawn,
the swords on the settles, and shields a-many
firm held in hand: nor helmet minded
nor harness of mail, whom that horror seized.
Haste was hers; she would hie afar
and save her life when the liegemen saw her.
Yet a single atheling up she seized
fast and firm, as she fled to the moor.
He was for Hrothgar of heroes the dearest,
of trusty vassals betwixt the seas,
whom she killed on his couch, a clansman famous,
in battle brave. Nor was Beowulf there;
another house had been held apart,
after giving of gold, for the Geat renowned.

Uproar filled Heorot; the hand all had viewed,
blood-flecked, she bore with her; bale was returned,
dole in the dwellings: 'twas dire exchange
where Dane and Geat were doomed to give
the lives of loved ones. Long-tried king,
the hoary hero, at heart was sad
when he knew his noble no more lived,
and dead indeed was his dearest thane.
To his bower was Beowulf brought in haste,
dauntless victor. As daylight broke,
along with his earls the atheling lord,
with his clansmen, came where the king abode
waiting to see if the Wielder-of-All
would turn this tale of trouble and woe.
Strode o'er floor the famed-in-strife,
with his hand-companions—the hall resounded—
wishing to greet the wise old king,
Ingwines' lord; he asked if the night
had passed in peace to the prince's mind.

20

Hrothgar spake, helmet-of-Scyldings:
"Ask not of pleasure! Pain is renewed
to Danish folk. Dead is Aeschere,
of Yrmenlaf the elder brother,
my sage adviser and stay in council,
shoulder-comrade in stress of fight
when warriors clashed and we warded our heads,
hewed the helm-boars; hero famed
should be every earl as Aeschere was!
But here in Heorot a hand hath slain him
of wandering death-sprite. I wot not whither,
proud of the prey, her path she took,
fain of her fill. The feud she avenged
that yesternight, unyieldingly,

Grendel in grimmest grasp thou killedst,
seeing how long these liegemen mine
he ruined and ravaged. Reft of life,
in arms he fell. Now another comes,
keen and cruel, her kin to avenge,
faring far in feud of blood:
so that many a thane shall think, who e'er
sorrows in soul for that sharer of rings,
this is hardest of heart-bales. The hand lies low
that once was willing each wish to please.
Land-dwellers here and liegemen mine,
who house by those parts, I have heard relate
that such a pair they have sometimes seen,
march-stalkers mighty the moorland haunting,
wandering spirits: one of them seemed,
so far as my folk could fairly judge,
of womankind; and one, accursed,
in man's guise trod the misery-track
of exile, though huger than human bulk.
Grendel in days long gone they named him,
folk of the land; his father they knew not,
nor any brood that was born to him
of treacherous spirits. Untrod is their home;
by wolf-cliffs haunt they and windy headlands,
fenways fearful, where flows the stream
from mountains gliding to gloom of the rocks,
underground flood. Not far is it hence
in measure of miles that the mere expands,
and o'er it the frost-bound forest hanging,
sturdily rooted, shadows the wave.
By night is a wonder weird to see,
fire on the waters. So wise lived none
of the sons of men, to search those depths!
Nay, though the heath-rover, harried by dogs,
the horn-proud hart, this holt should seek,
long distance driven, his dear life first
on the brink he yields ere he brave the plunge
to hide his head: 'tis no happy place!
Thence the welter of waters washes up

wan to welkin when winds bestir
evil storms, and air grows dusk,
and the heavens weep. Now is help once more
with thee alone! The land thou knowst not,
place of fear, where thou findest out
that sin-flecked being. Seek if thou dare!
I will reward thee, for waging this fight,
with ancient treasure, as erst I did,
with winding gold, if thou winnest back."

21

Beowulf spake, bairn of Ecgtheow:
"Sorrow not, sage! It beseems us better
friends to avenge than fruitlessly mourn them.
Each of us all must his end abide
in the ways of the world; so win who may
glory ere death! When his days are told,
that is the warrior's worthiest doom.
Rise, O realm-warder! Ride we anon,
and mark the trail of the mother of Grendel.
No harbor shall hide her—heed my promise!—
enfolding of field or forested mountain
or floor of the flood, let her flee where she will!
But thou this day endure in patience,
as I ween thou wilt, thy woes each one."
Leaped up the graybeard: God he thanked,
mighty Lord, for the man's brave words.
For Hrothgar soon a horse was saddled
wave-maned steed. The sovran wise
stately rode on; his shield-armed men
followed in force. The footprints led
along the woodland, widely seen,
a path o'er the plain, where she passed, and trod
the murky moor; of men-at-arms
she bore the bravest and best one, dead,

him who with Hrothgar the homestead ruled.
On then went the atheling-born
o'er stone-cliffs steep and strait defiles,
narrow passes and unknown ways,
headlands sheer, and the haunts of the nicors.
Foremost he fared, a few at his side
of the wiser men, the ways to scan,
till he found in a flash the forested hill
hanging over the hoary rock,
a woeful wood: the waves below
were dyed in blood. The Danish men
had sorrow of soul, and for Scyldings all,
for many a hero, 'twas hard to bear,
ill for earls, when Aeschere's head
they found by the flood on the foreland there.
Waves were welling, the warriors saw,
hot with blood; but the horn sang oft
battle-song bold. The band sat down,
and watched on the water worm-like things,
sea-dragons strange that sounded the deep,
and nicors that lay on the ledge of the ness—
such as oft essay at hour of morn
on the road-of-sails their ruthless quest—
and sea-snakes and monsters. These started away,
swollen and savage that song to hear,
that war-horn's blast. The warden of Geats,
with bolt from bow, then balked of life,
of wave-work, one monster, amid its heart
went the keen war-shaft; in water it seemed
less doughty in swimming whom death had seized.
Swift on the billows, with boar-spears well
hooked and barbed, it was hard beset,
done to death and dragged on the headland,
wave-roamer wondrous. Warriors viewed
the grisly guest. Then girt him Beowulf
in martial mail, nor mourned for his life.
His breastplate broad and bright of hues,
woven by hand, should the waters try;
well could it ward the warrior's body
that battle should break on his breast in vain

nor harm his heart by the hand of a foe.
And the helmet white that his head protected
was destined to dare the deeps of the flood,
through wave-whirl win: 'twas wound with chains,
decked with gold, as in days of yore
the weapon-smith worked it wondrously,
with swine-forms set it, that swords nowise,
brandished in battle, could bite that helm.
Nor was that the meanest of mighty helps
which Hrothgar's orator offered at need:
"Hrunting" they named the hilted sword,
of old-time heirlooms easily first;
iron was its edge, all etched with poison,
with battle-blood hardened, nor blenched it at fight
in hero's hand who held it ever,
on paths of peril prepared to go
to folkstead of foes. Not first time this
it was destined to do a daring task.
For he bore not in mind, the bairn of Ecglaf
sturdy and strong, that speech he had made,
drunk with wine, now this weapon he lent
to a stouter swordsman. Himself, though, durst not
under welter of waters wager his life
as loyal liegeman. So lost he his glory,
honor of earls. With the other not so,
who girded him now for the grim encounter.

22

Beowulf spake, bairn of Ecgtheow:
"Have mind, thou honored offspring of Healfdene
gold-friend of men, now I go on this quest,
sovran wise, what once was said:
if in thy cause it came that I
should lose my life, thou wouldst loyal bide
to me, though fallen, in father's place!
Be guardian, thou, to this group of my thanes,

my warrior-friends, if War should seize me;
and the goodly gifts thou gavest me,
Hrothgar beloved, to Hygelac send!
Geatland's king may ken by the gold,
Hrethel's son see, when he stares at the treasure,
that I got me a friend for goodness famed,
and joyed while I could in my jewel-bestower.
And let Unferth wield this wondrous sword,
earl far-honored, this heirloom precious,
hard of edge: with Hrunting I
seek doom of glory, or Death shall take me."

After these words the Weder-Geat lord
boldly hastened, biding never
answer at all: the ocean floods
closed o'er the hero. Long while of the day
fled ere he felt the floor of the sea.

Soon found the fiend who the flood-domain
sword-hungry held these hundred winters,
greedy and grim, that some guest from above,
some man, was raiding her monster-realm.
She grasped out for him with grisly claws,
and the warrior seized; yet scathed she not
his body hale; the breastplate hindered,
as she strove to shatter the sark of war,
the linked harness, with loathsome hand.
Then bore this brine-wolf, when bottom she touched,
the lord of rings to the lair she haunted
whiles vainly he strove, though his valor held,
weapon to wield against wondrous monsters
that sore beset him; sea-beasts many
tried with fierce tusks to tear his mail,
and swarmed on the stranger. But soon he marked
he was now in some hall, he knew not which,
where water never could work him harm,
nor through the roof could reach him ever
fangs of the flood. Firelight he saw,
beams of a blaze that brightly shone.

Then the warrior was ware of that wolf-of-the-deep,
mere-wife monstrous. For mighty stroke
he swung his blade, and the blow withheld not.
Then sang on her head that seemly blade
its war-song wild. But the warrior found
the light-of-battle was loath to bite,
to harm the heart: its hard edge failed
the noble at need, yet had known of old
strife hand to hand, and had helmets cloven,
doomed men's fighting-gear. First time, this,
for the gleaming blade that its glory fell.
Firm still stood, nor failed in valor,
heedful of high deeds, Hygelac's kinsman;
flung away fretted sword, featly jewelled,
the angry earl; on earth it lay
steel-edged and stiff. His strength he trusted,
hand-gripe of might. So man shall do
whenever in war he weens to earn him
lasting fame, nor fears for his life!
Seized then by shoulder, shrank not from combat,
the Geatish war-prince Grendel's mother.
Flung then the fierce one, filled with wrath,
his deadly foe, that she fell to ground.
Swift on her part she paid him back
with grisly grasp, and grappled with him.
Spent with struggle, stumbled the warrior,
fiercest of fighting-men, fell adown.
On the hall-guest she hurled herself, hent her short sword,
broad and brown-edged, the bairn to avenge,
the sole-born son. On his shoulder lay
braided breast-mail, barring death,
withstanding entrance of edge or blade.
Life would have ended for Ecgtheow's son,
under wide earth for that earl of Geats,
had his armor of war not aided him,
battle-net hard, and holy God
wielded the victory, wisest Maker.
The Lord of Heaven allowed his cause;
and easily rose the earl erect.

23

'Mid the battle-gear saw he a blade triumphant,
old-sword of Eotens, with edge of proof,
warriors' heirloom, weapon unmatched—
save only 'twas more than other men
to bandy-of-battle could bear at all—
as the giants had wrought it, ready and keen.
Seized then its chain-hilt the Scyldings' chieftain,
bold and battle-grim, brandished the sword,
reckless of life, and so wrathfully smote
that it gripped her neck and grasped her hard,
her bone-rings breaking: the blade pierced through
that fated-one's flesh: to floor she sank.
Bloody the blade: he was blithe of his deed.
Then blazed forth light. 'Twas bright within
as when from the sky there shines unclouded
heaven's candle. The hall he scanned.
By the wall then went he; his weapon raised
high by its hilts the Hygelac-thane,
angry and eager. That edge was not useless
to the warrior now. He wished with speed
Grendel to guerdon for grim raids many,
for the war he waged on Western-Danes
oftener far than an only time,
when of Hrothgar's hearth-companions
he slew in slumber, in sleep devoured,
fifteen men of the folk of Danes,
and as many others outward bore,
his horrible prey. Well paid for that
the wrathful prince! For now prone he saw
Grendel stretched there, spent with war,
spoiled of life, so scathed had left him
Heorot's battle. The body sprang far
when after death it endured the blow,
sword-stroke savage, that severed its head.
Soon, then, saw the sage companions
who waited with Hrothgar, watching the flood,
that the tossing waters turbid grew,

blood-stained the mere. Old men together,
hoary-haired, of the hero spake;
the warrior would not, they weened, again,
proud of conquest, come to seek
their mighty master. To many it seemed
the wolf-of-the-waves had won his life.
The ninth hour came. The noble Scyldings
left the headland; homeward went
the gold-friend of men. But the guests sat on,
stared at the surges, sick in heart,
and wished, yet weened not, their winsome lord
again to see. Now that sword began,
from blood of the fight, in battle-droppings,
war-blade, to wane: 'twas a wondrous thing
that all of it melted as ice is wont
when frosty fetters the Father loosens,
unwinds the wave-bonds, wielding all
seasons and times: the true God he!
Nor took from that dwelling the duke of the Geats
save only the head and that hilt withal
blazoned with jewels: the blade had melted,
burned was the bright sword, her blood was so hot,
so poisoned the hell-sprite who perished within there.
Soon he was swimming who safe saw in combat
downfall of demons; up-dove through the flood.
The clashing waters were cleansed now,
waste of waves, where the wandering fiend
her life-days left and this lapsing world.
Swam then to strand the sailors'-refuge,
sturdy-in-spirit, of sea-booty glad,
of burden brave he bore with him.
Went then to greet him, and God they thanked,
the thane-band choice of their chieftain blithe,
that safe and sound they could see him again.
Soon from the hardy one helmet and armor
deftly they doffed: now drowsed the mere,
water 'neath welkin, with war-blood stained.
Forth they fared by the footpaths thence,
merry at heart the highways measured,

well-known roads. Courageous men
carried the head from the cliff by the sea,
an arduous task for all the band,
the firm in fight, since four were needed
on the shaft-of-slaughter strenuously
to bear to the gold-hall Grendel's head.
So presently to the palace there
foemen fearless, fourteen Geats,
marching came. Their master-of-clan
mighty amid them the meadow-ways trod.
Strode then within the sovran thane
fearless in fight, of fame renowned,
hardy hero, Hrothgar to greet.
And next by the hair into hall was borne
Grendel's head, where the henchmen were drinking,
an awe to clan and queen alike,
a monster of marvel: the men looked on.

24

Beowulf spake, bairn of Ecgtheow:
"Lo, now, this sea-booty, son of Healfdene,
Lord of Scyldings, we've lustily brought thee,
sign of glory; thou seest it here.
Not lightly did I with my life escape!
In war under water this work I essayed
with endless effort; and even so
my strength had been lost had the Lord not shielded me.
Not a whit could I with Hrunting do
in work of war, though the weapon is good;
yet a sword the Sovran of Men vouchsafed me
to spy on the wall there, in splendor hanging,
old, gigantic—how oft He guides
the friendless wight!—and I fought with that brand,
felling in fight, since fate was with me,
the house's wardens. That war-sword then

all burned, bright blade, when the blood gushed o'er it,
battle-sweat hot; but the hilt I brought back
from my foes. So avenged I their fiendish deeds
death-fall of Danes, as was due and right.
And this is my hest, that in Heorot now
safe thou canst sleep with thy soldier band,
and every thane of all thy folk
both old and young; no evil fear,
Scyldings' lord, from that side again,
aught ill for thy earls, as erst thou must!"
Then the golden hilt, for that gray-haired leader,
hoary hero, in hand was laid,
giant-wrought, old. So owned and enjoyed it
after downfall of devils, the Danish lord,
wonder-smiths' work, since the world was rid
of that grim-souled fiend, the foe of God,
murder-marked, and his mother as well.
Now it passed into power of the people's king,
best of all that the oceans bound
who have scattered their gold o'er Scandia's isle.
Hrothgar spake—the hilt he viewed,
heirloom old, where was etched the rise
of that far-off fight when the floods o'erwhelmed,
raging waves, the race of giants
(fearful their fate!), a folk estranged
from God Eternal: whence guerdon due
in that waste of waters the Wielder paid them.
So on the guard of shining gold
in runic staves it was rightly said
for whom the serpent-traced sword was wrought,
best of blades, in bygone days,
and the hilt well wound. The wise one spake,
son of Healfdene; silent were all:
"Lo, so may he say who sooth and right
follows 'mid folk, of far times mindful,
a land-warden old, that this earl belongs
to the better breed! So, borne aloft,
thy fame must fly, O friend my Beowulf,
far and wide o'er folksteads many. Firmly thou

shalt all maintain, mighty strength with mood of wisdom.
Love of mine will I assure thee,
as, awhile ago, I promised; thou shalt prove a stay
in future, in far-off years, to folk of thine,
to the heroes a help. Was not Heremod thus
to offspring of Ecgwela, Honor-Scyldings,
nor grew for their grace, but for grisly slaughter,
for doom of death to the Danishmen.

He slew, wrath-swollen, his shoulder-comrades,
companions at board! So he passed alone,
chieftain haughty, from human cheer.
Though him the Maker with might endowed,
delights of power, and uplifted high
above all men, yet blood-fierce his mind,
his breast-hoard, grew, no bracelets gave he
to Danes as was due; he endured all joyless
strain of struggle and stress of woe,
long feud with his folk. Here find thy lesson!
Of virtue advise thee! This verse I have said for thee,
wise from lapsed winters. Wondrous seems
how to sons of men Almighty God
in the strength of His spirit sendeth wisdom,
estate, high station: He swayeth all things.
Whiles He letteth right lustily fare
the heart of the hero of high-born race,
in seat ancestral assigns him bliss,
his folk's sure fortress in fee to hold,
puts in his power great parts of the earth,
empire so ample, that end of it
this wanter-of-wisdom weeneth none.
So he waxes in wealth, nowise can harm him
illness or age; no evil cares
shadow his spirit; no sword-hate threatens
from ever an enemy: all the world
wends at his will, no worse he knoweth,
till all within him obstinate pride
waxes and wakes while the warden slumbers,
the spirit's sentry; sleep is too fast

which masters his might, and the murderer nears,
stealthily shooting the shafts from his bow!"

25

"Under harness his heart then is hit indeed
by sharpest shafts; and no shelter avails
from foul behest of the hellish fiend.
Him seems too little what long he possessed.
Greedy and grim, no golden rings
he gives for his pride; the promised future
forgets he and spurns, with all God has sent him,
Wonder-Wielder, of wealth and fame.
Yet in the end it ever comes
that the frame of the body fragile yields,
fated falls; and there follows another
who joyously the jewels divides,
the royal riches, nor recks of his forebear.
Ban, then, such baleful thoughts, Beowulf dearest,
best of men, and the better part choose,
profit eternal; and temper thy pride,
warrior famous! The flower of thy might
lasts now a while: but erelong it shall be
that sickness or sword thy strength shall minish,
or fang of fire, or flooding billow,
or bite of blade, or brandished spear,
or odious age; or the eyes' clear beam
wax dull and darken: Death even thee
in haste shall o'erwhelm, thou hero of war!
So the Ring-Danes these half-years a hundred I ruled,
wielded 'neath welkin, and warded them bravely
from mighty-ones many o'er middle-earth,
from spear and sword, till it seemed for me
no foe could be found under fold of the sky.
Lo, sudden the shift! To me seated secure
came grief for joy when Grendel began

to harry my home, the hellish foe;
for those ruthless raids, unresting I suffered
heart-sorrow heavy. Heaven be thanked,
Lord Eternal, for life extended
that I on this head all hewn and bloody,
after long evil, with eyes may gaze!
Go to the bench now! Be glad at banquet,
warrior worthy! A wealth of treasure
at dawn of day, be dealt between us!"
Glad was the Geats' lord, going betimes
to seek his seat, as the Sage commanded.
Afresh, as before, for the famed-in-battle,
for the band of the hall, was a banquet dight
nobly anew. The Night-Helm darkened
dusk o'er the drinkers. The doughty ones rose:
for the hoary-headed would hasten to rest,
aged Scylding; and eager the Geat,
shield-fighter sturdy, for sleeping yearned.
Him wander-weary, warrior-guest
from far, a hall-thane heralded forth,
who by custom courtly cared for all
needs of a thane as in those old days
warrior-wanderers wont to have.
So slumbered the stout-heart. Stately the hall
rose gabled and gilt where the guest slept on
till a raven black the rapture-of-heaven
blithe-heart boded. Bright came flying
shine after shadow. The swordsmen hastened,
athelings all were eager homeward
forth to fare; and far from thence
the great-hearted guest would guide his keel.
Bade then the hardy one Hrunting be brought
to the son of Ecglaf, the sword bade him take,
excellent iron, and uttered his thanks for it,
quoth that he counted it keen in battle,
"war-friend" winsome: with words he slandered not
edge of the blade: 'twas a big-hearted man!
Now eager for parting and armed at point
warriors waited, while went to his host

that Darling of Danes. The doughty atheling
to high-seat hastened and Hrothgar greeted.

26

Beowulf spake, bairn of Ecgtheow:
"Lo, we seafarers say our will,
far-come men, that we fain would seek
Hygelac now. We here have found
hosts to our heart: thou hast harbored us well.
If ever on earth I am able to win me
more of thy love, O lord of men,
aught anew, than I now have done,
for work of war I am willing still!
If it come to me ever across the seas
that neighbor foemen annoy and fright thee—
as they that hate thee erewhile have used—
thousands then of thanes I shall bring,
heroes to help thee. Of Hygelac I know,
ward of his folk, that, though few his years,
the lord of the Geats will give me aid
by word and by work, that well I may serve thee,
wielding the war-wood to win thy triumph
and lending thee might when thou lackest men.
If thy Hrethric should come to court of Geats,
a sovran's son, he will surely there
find his friends. A far-off land
each man should visit who vaunts him brave."
Him then answering, Hrothgar spake:
"These words of thine the wisest God
sent to thy soul! No sager counsel
from so young in years e'er yet have I heard.
Thou art strong of main and in mind art wary,
art wise in words! I ween indeed
if ever it hap that Hrethel's heir

by spear be seized, by sword-grim battle,
by illness or iron, thine elder and lord,
people's leader—and life be thine—
no seemlier man will the Sea-Geats find
at all to choose for their chief and king,
for hoard-guard of heroes, if hold thou wilt
thy kinsman's kingdom! Thy keen mind pleases me
the longer the better, Beowulf loved!

Thou hast brought it about that both our peoples,
sons of the Geat and Spear-Dane folk,
shall have mutual peace, and from murderous strife,
such as once they waged, from war refrain.
Long as I rule this realm so wide,
let our hoards be common, let heroes with gold
each other greet o'er the gannet's-bath,
and the ringed-prow bear o'er rolling waves
tokens of love. I trow my landfolk
towards friend and foe are firmly joined,
and honor they keep in the olden way."
To him in the hall, then, Healfdene's son
gave treasures twelve, and the trust-of-earls
bade him fare with the gifts to his folk beloved,
hale to his home, and in haste return.
Then kissed the king of kin renowned,
Scyldings' chieftain, that choicest thane,
and fell on his neck. Fast flowed the tears
of the hoary-headed. Heavy with winters,
he had chances twain, but he clung to this,
that each should look on the other again,
and hear him in hall. Was this hero so dear to him.
his breast's wild billows he banned in vain;
safe in his soul a secret longing,
locked in his mind, for that loved man
burned in his blood. Then Beowulf strode,
glad of his gold-gifts, the grass-plot o'er,
warrior blithe. The wave-roamer bode
riding at anchor, its owner awaiting.
As they hastened onward, Hrothgar's gift

they lauded at length. 'Twas a lord unpeered,
every way blameless, till age had broken—
it spareth no mortal—his splendid might.

27

Came now to ocean the ever-courageous
hardy henchmen, their harness bearing,
woven war-sarks. The warden marked,
trusty as ever, the earl's return.
From the height of the hill no hostile words
reached the guests as he rode to greet them;
but "Welcome!" he called to that Weder clan
as the sheen-mailed spoilers to ship marched on.
Then on the strand, with steeds and treasure
and armor their roomy and ring-dight ship
was heavily laden: high its mast
rose over Hrothgar's hoarded gems.
A sword to the boat-guard Beowulf gave,
mounted with gold; on the mead-bench since
he was better esteemed, that blade possessing,
heirloom old. Their ocean-keel boarding,
they drove through the deep, and Daneland left.
A sea-cloth was set, a sail with ropes,
firm to the mast; the flood-timbers moaned;
nor did wind over billows that wave-swimmer blow
across from her course. The craft sped on,
foam-necked it floated forth o'er the waves,
keel firm-bound over briny currents,
till they got them sight of the Geatish cliffs,
home-known headlands. High the boat,
stirred by winds, on the strand updrove.
Helpful at haven the harbor-guard stood,
who long already for loved companions
by the water had waited and watched afar.
He bound to the beach the broad-bosomed ship

with anchor-bands, lest ocean-billows
that trusty timber should tear away.
Then Beowulf bade them bear the treasure,
gold and jewels; no journey far
was it thence to go to the giver of rings,
Hygelac Hrethling: at home he dwelt
by the sea-wall close, himself and clan.
Haughty that house, a hero the king,
high the hall, and Hygd right young,
wise and wary, though winters few
in those fortress walls she had found a home,
Haereth's daughter. Nor humble her ways,
nor grudged she gifts to the Geatish men,
of precious treasure. Not Thryth's pride showed she,
folk-queen famed, or that fell deceit.
Was none so daring that durst make bold
(save her lord alone) of the liegemen dear
that lady full in the face to look,
but forged fetters he found his lot,
bonds of death! And brief the respite;
soon as they seized him, his sword-doom was spoken,
and the burnished blade a baleful murder
proclaimed and closed. No queenly way
for woman to practise, though peerless she,
that the weaver-of-peace from warrior dear
by wrath and lying his life should reave!
But Hemming's kinsman hindered this.
For over their ale men also told
that of these folk-horrors fewer she wrought,
onslaughts of evil, after she went,
gold-decked bride, to the brave young prince,
atheling haughty, and Offa's hall
o'er the fallow flood at her father's bidding
safely sought, where since she prospered,
royal, throned, rich in goods,
fain of the fair life fate had sent her,
and leal in love to the lord of warriors.
He, of all heroes I heard of ever
from sea to sea, of the sons of earth,

most excellent seemed. Hence Offa was praised
for his fighting and feeing by far-off men,
the spear-bold warrior; wisely he ruled
over his empire. Eomer woke to him,
help of heroes, Hemming's kinsman,
Grandson of Garmund, grim in war.

28

Hastened the hardy one, henchmen with him,
sandy strand of the sea to tread
and widespread ways. The world's great candle,
sun shone from south. They strode along
with sturdy steps to the spot they knew
where the battle-king young, his burg within,
slayer of Ongentheow, shared the rings,
shelter-of-heroes. To Hygelac
Beowulf's coming was quickly told,
that there in the court the clansmen's refuge,
the shield-companion sound and alive,
hale from the hero-play homeward strode.
With haste in the hall, by highest order,
room for the rovers was readily made.
By his sovran he sat, come safe from battle,
kinsman by kinsman. His kindly lord
he first had greeted in gracious form,
with manly words. The mead dispensing,
came through the high hall Haereth's daughter,
winsome to warriors, wine-cup bore
to the hands of the heroes. Hygelac then
his comrade fairly with question plied
in the lofty hall, sore longing to know
what manner of sojourn the Sea-Geats made.
"What came of thy quest, my kinsman Beowulf,
when thy yearnings suddenly swept thee yonder
battle to seek o'er the briny sea,

combat in Heorot? Hrothgar couldst thou
aid at all, the honored chief,
in his wide-known woes? With waves of care
my sad heart seethed; I sore mistrusted
my loved one's venture: long I begged thee
by no means to seek that slaughtering monster,
but suffer the South-Danes to settle their feud
themselves with Grendel. Now God be thanked
that safe and sound I can see thee now!"
Beowulf spake, the bairn of Ecgtheow:
"'Tis known and unhidden, Hygelac Lord,
to many men, that meeting of ours,
struggle grim between Grendel and me,
which we fought on the field where full too many
sorrows he wrought for the Scylding-Victors,
evils unending. These all I avenged.
No boast can be from breed of Grendel,
any on earth, for that uproar at dawn,
from the longest-lived of the loathsome race
in fleshly fold! But first I went
Hrothgar to greet in the hall of gifts,
where Healfdene's kinsman high-renowned,
soon as my purpose was plain to him,
assigned me a seat by his son and heir.
The liegemen were lusty; my life-days never
such merry men over mead in hall
have I heard under heaven! The high-born queen,
people's peace-bringer, passed through the hall,
cheered the young clansmen, clasps of gold,
ere she sought her seat, to sundry gave.
Oft to the heroes Hrothgar's daughter,
to earls in turn, the ale-cup tendered—
she whom I heard these hall-companions
Freawaru name, when fretted gold
she proffered the warriors. Promised is she,
gold-decked maid, to the glad son of Froda.
Sage this seems to the Scylding's-friend,
kingdom's-keeper: he counts it wise
the woman to wed so and ward off feud,

store of slaughter. But seldom ever
when men are slain, does the murder-spear sink
but briefest while, though the bride be fair!
"Nor haply will like it the Heathobard lord,
and as little each of his liegemen all,
when a thane of the Danes, in that doughty throng,
goes with the lady along their hall,
and on him the old-time heirlooms glisten
hard and ring-decked, Heathobard's treasure,
weapons that once they wielded fair
until they lost at the linden-play
liegeman leal and their lives as well.
Then, over the ale, on this heirloom gazing,
some ash-wielder old who has all in mind
that spear-death of men—he is stern of mood,
heavy at heart—in the hero young
tests the temper and tries the soul
and war-hate wakens, with words like these:
"Canst thou not, comrade, ken that sword
which to the fray thy father carried
in his final feud, 'neath the fighting-mask,
dearest of blades, when the Danish slew him
and wielded the war-place on Withergild's fall,
after havoc of heroes, those hardy Scyldings?
Now, the son of a certain slaughtering Dane,
proud of his treasure, paces this hall,
joys in the killing, and carries the jewel
that rightfully ought to be owned by thee!"
Thus he urges and eggs him all the time
with keenest words, till occasion offers
that Freawaru's thane, for his father's deed,
after bite of brand in his blood must slumber,
losing his life; but that liegeman flies
living away, for the land he kens.
And thus be broken on both their sides
oaths of the earls, when Ingeld's breast
wells with war-hate, and wife-love now
after the care-billows cooler grows.
"So I hold not high the Heathobards' faith

due to the Danes, or their during love
and pact of peace. But I pass from that,
turning to Grendel, O giver-of-treasure,
and saying in full how the fight resulted,
hand-fray of heroes. When heaven's jewel
had fled o'er far fields, that fierce sprite came,
night-foe savage, to seek us out
where safe and sound we sentried the hall.
To Hondscio then was that harassing deadly,
his fall there was fated. He first was slain,
girded warrior. Grendel on him
turned murderous mouth, on our mighty kinsman,
and all of the brave man's body devoured.
Yet none the earlier, empty-handed,
would the bloody-toothed murderer, mindful of bale,
outward go from the gold-decked hall:
but me he attacked in his terror of might,
with greedy hand grasped me. A glove hung by him
wide and wondrous, wound with bands;
and in artful wise it all was wrought,
by devilish craft, of dragon-skins.
Me therein, an innocent man,
the fiendish foe was fain to thrust
with many another. He might not so,
when I all angrily upright stood.
'Twere long to relate how that land-destroyer
I paid in kind for his cruel deeds;
yet there, my prince, this people of thine
got fame by my fighting. He fled away,
and a little space his life preserved;
but there staid behind him his stronger hand
left in Heorot; heartsick thence
on the floor of the ocean that outcast fell.
Me for this struggle the Scyldings'-friend
paid in plenty with plates of gold,
with many a treasure, when morn had come
and we all at the banquet-board sat down.
Then was song and glee. The gray-haired Scylding,

much tested, told of the times of yore.
Whiles the hero his harp bestirred,
wood-of-delight; now lays he chanted
of sooth and sadness, or said aright
legends of wonder, the wide-hearted king;
or for years of his youth he would yearn at times,
for strength of old struggles, now stricken with age,
hoary hero: his heart surged full
when, wise with winters, he wailed their flight.
Thus in the hall the whole of that day
at ease we feasted, till fell o'er earth
another night. Anon full ready
in greed of vengeance, Grendel's mother
set forth all doleful. Dead was her son
through war-hate of Weders; now, woman monstrous
with fury fell a foeman she slew,
avenged her offspring. From Aeschere old,
loyal councillor, life was gone;
nor might they e'en, when morning broke,
those Danish people, their death-done comrade
burn with brands, on balefire lay
the man they mourned. Under mountain stream
she had carried the corpse with cruel hands.
For Hrothgar that was the heaviest sorrow
of all that had laden the lord of his folk.
The leader then, by thy life, besought me
(sad was his soul) in the sea-waves' coil
to play the hero and hazard my being
for glory of prowess: my guerdon he pledged.
I then in the waters—'tis widely known—
that sea-floor-guardian savage found.
Hand-to-hand there a while we struggled;
billows welled blood; in the briny hall
her head I hewed with a hardy blade
from Grendel's mother—and gained my life,
though not without danger. My doom was not yet.
Then the haven-of-heroes, Healfdene's son,
gave me in guerdon great gifts of price."

29

"So held this king to the customs old,
that I wanted for nought in the wage I gained,
the meed of my might; he made me gifts,
Healfdene's heir, for my own disposal.
Now to thee, my prince, I proffer them all,
gladly give them. Thy grace alone
can find me favor. Few indeed
have I of kinsmen, save, Hygelac, thee!"
Then he bade them bear him the boar-head standard,
the battle-helm high, and breastplate gray,
the splendid sword; then spake in form:
"Me this war-gear the wise old prince,
Hrothgar, gave, and his hest he added,
that its story be straightway said to thee.
A while it was held by Heorogar king,
for long time lord of the land of Scyldings;
yet not to his son the sovran left it,
to daring Heoroweard, dear as he was to him,
his harness of battle. Well hold thou it all!"
And I heard that soon passed o'er the path of this treasure,
all apple-fallow, four good steeds,
each like the others, arms and horses
he gave to the king. So should kinsmen be,
not weave one another the net of wiles,
or with deep-hid treachery death contrive
for neighbor and comrade. His nephew was ever
by hardy Hygelac held full dear,
and each kept watch o'er the other's weal.
I heard, too, the necklace to Hygd he presented,
wonder-wrought treasure, which Wealhtheow gave him
sovran's daughter: three steeds he added,
slender and saddle-gay. Since such gift
the gem gleamed bright on the breast of the queen.
Thus showed his strain the son of Ecgtheow
as a man remarked for mighty deeds
and acts of honor. At ale he slew not
comrade or kin; nor cruel his mood,

though of sons of earth his strength was greatest,
a glorious gift that God had sent
the splendid leader. Long was he spurned,
and worthless by Geatish warriors held;
him at mead the master-of-clans
failed full oft to favor at all.
Slack and shiftless the strong men deemed him,
profitless prince; but payment came,
to the warrior honored, for all his woes.
Then the bulwark-of-earls bade bring within,
hardy chieftain, Hrethel's heirloom
garnished with gold: no Geat e'er knew
in shape of a sword a statelier prize.
The brand he laid in Beowulf's lap;
and of hides assigned him seven thousand,
with house and high-seat. They held in common
land alike by their line of birth,
inheritance, home: but higher the king
because of his rule o'er the realm itself.

Now further it fell with the flight of years,
with harryings horrid, that Hygelac perished,
and Heardred, too, by hewing of swords
under the shield-wall slaughtered lay,
when him at the van of his victor-folk
sought hardy heroes, Heatho-Scylfings,
in arms o'erwhelming Hereric's nephew.
Then Beowulf came as king this broad
realm to wield; and he ruled it well
fifty winters, a wise old prince,
warding his land, until One began
in the dark of night, a Dragon, to rage.
In the grave on the hill a hoard it guarded,
in the stone-barrow steep. A strait path reached it,
unknown to mortals. Some man, however,
came by chance that cave within
to the heathen hoard. In hand he took
a golden goblet, nor gave he it back,
stole with it away, while the watcher slept,

by thievish wiles: for the warden's wrath
prince and people must pay betimes!

30

That way he went with no will of his own,
in danger of life, to the dragon's hoard,
but for pressure of peril, some prince's thane.
He fled in fear the fatal scourge,
seeking shelter, a sinful man,
and entered in. At the awful sight
tottered that guest, and terror seized him;
yet the wretched fugitive rallied anon
from fright and fear ere he fled away,
and took the cup from that treasure-hoard.
Of such besides there was store enough,
heirlooms old, the earth below,
which some earl forgotten, in ancient years,
left the last of his lofty race,
heedfully there had hidden away,
dearest treasure. For death of yore
had hurried all hence; and he alone
left to live, the last of the clan,
weeping his friends, yet wished to bide
warding the treasure, his one delight,
though brief his respite. The barrow, new-ready,
to strand and sea-waves stood anear,
hard by the headland, hidden and closed;
there laid within it his lordly heirlooms
and heaped hoard of heavy gold
that warden of rings. Few words he spake:
"Now hold thou, earth, since heroes may not,
what earls have owned! Lo, erst from thee
brave men brought it! But battle-death seized
and cruel killing my clansmen all,
robbed them of life and a liegeman's joys.
None have I left to lift the sword,

or to cleanse the carven cup of price,
beaker bright. My brave are gone.
And the helmet hard, all haughty with gold,
shall part from its plating. Polishers sleep
who could brighten and burnish the battle-mask;
and those weeds of war that were wont to brave
over bicker of shields the bite of steel
rust with their bearer. The ringed mail
fares not far with famous chieftain,
at side of hero! No harp's delight,
no glee-wood's gladness! No good hawk now
flies through the hall! Nor horses fleet
stamp in the burgstead! Battle and death
the flower of my race have reft away."
Mournful of mood, thus he moaned his woe,
alone, for them all, and unblithe wept
by day and by night, till death's fell wave
o'erwhelmed his heart. His hoard-of-bliss
that old ill-doer open found,
who, blazing at twilight the barrows haunteth,
naked foe-dragon flying by night
folded in fire: the folk of earth
dread him sore. 'Tis his doom to seek
hoard in the graves, and heathen gold
to watch, many-wintered: nor wins he thereby!
Powerful this plague-of-the-people thus
held the house of the hoard in earth
three hundred winters; till One aroused
wrath in his breast, to the ruler bearing
that costly cup, and the king implored
for bond of peace. So the barrow was plundered,
borne off was booty. His boon was granted
that wretched man; and his ruler saw
first time what was fashioned in far-off days.
When the dragon awoke, new woe was kindled.
O'er the stone he snuffed. The stark-heart found
footprint of foe who so far had gone
in his hidden craft by the creature's head.
So may the undoomed easily flee
evils and exile, if only he gain

the grace of the Wielder! That warden of gold
o'er the ground went seeking, greedy to find
the man who wrought him such wrong in sleep.
Savage and burning, the barrow he circled
all without; nor was any there,
none in the waste. Yet war he desired,
was eager for battle. The barrow he entered,
sought the cup, and discovered soon
that some one of mortals had searched his treasure,
his lordly gold. The guardian waited
ill-enduring till evening came;
boiling with wrath was the barrow's keeper,
and fain with flame the foe to pay
for the dear cup's loss. Now day was fled
as the worm had wished. By its wall no more
was it glad to bide, but burning flew
folded in flame: a fearful beginning
for sons of the soil; and soon it came,
in the doom of their lord, to a dreadful end.

31

Then the baleful fiend its fire belched out,
and bright homes burned. The blaze stood high
all landsfolk frighting. No living thing
would that loathly one leave as aloft it flew.
Wide was the dragon's warring seen,
its fiendish fury far and near,
as the grim destroyer those Geatish people
hated and hounded. To hidden lair,
to its hoard it hastened at hint of dawn.
Folk of the land it had lapped in flame,
with bale and brand. In its barrow it trusted,
its battling and bulwarks: that boast was vain!

To Beowulf then the bale was told
quickly and truly: the king's own home,

of buildings the best, in brand-waves melted,
that gift-throne of Geats. To the good old man
sad in heart, 'twas heaviest sorrow.
The sage assumed that his sovran God
he had angered, breaking ancient law,
and embittered the Lord. His breast within
with black thoughts welled, as his wont was never.
The folk's own fastness that fiery dragon
with flame had destroyed, and the stronghold all
washed by waves; but the warlike king,
prince of the Weders, plotted vengeance.
Warriors'-bulwark, he bade them work
all of iron—the earl's commander—
a war-shield wondrous: well he knew
that forest-wood against fire were worthless,
linden could aid not. Atheling brave,
he was fated to finish this fleeting life,
his days on earth, and the dragon with him,
though long it had watched o'er the wealth of the hoard!
Shame he reckoned it, sharer-of-rings,
to follow the flyer-afar with a host,
a broad-flung band; nor the battle feared he,
nor deemed he dreadful the dragon's warring,
its vigor and valor: ventures desperate
he had passed a-plenty, and perils of war,
contest-crash, since, conqueror proud,
Hrothgar's hall he had wholly purged,
and in grapple had killed the kin of Grendel,
loathsome breed! Not least was that
of hand-to-hand fights where Hygelac fell,
when the ruler of Geats in rush of battle,
lord of his folk, in the Frisian land,
son of Hrethel, by sword-draughts died,
by brands down-beaten. Thence Beowulf fled
through strength of himself and his swimming power,
though alone, and his arms were laden with thirty
coats of mail, when he came to the sea!
Nor yet might Hetwaras haughtily boast
their craft of contest, who carried against him
shields to the fight: but few escaped

from strife with the hero to seek their homes!
Then swam over ocean Ecgtheow's son
lonely and sorrowful, seeking his land,
where Hygd made him offer of hoard and realm,
rings and royal-seat, reckoning naught
the strength of her son to save their kingdom
from hostile hordes, after Hygelac's death.
No sooner for this could the stricken ones
in any wise move that atheling's mind
over young Heardred's head as lord
and ruler of all the realm to be:
yet the hero upheld him with helpful words,
aided in honor, till, older grown,
he wielded the Weder-Geats. Wandering exiles
sought him o'er seas, the sons of Ohtere,
who had spurned the sway of the Scylfings'-helmet,
the bravest and best that broke the rings,
in Swedish land, of the sea-kings' line,
haughty hero. Hence Heardred's end.
For shelter he gave them, sword-death came,
the blade's fell blow, to bairn of Hygelac;
but the son of Ongentheow sought again
house and home when Heardred fell,
leaving Beowulf lord of Geats
and gift-seat's master. A good king he!

32

The fall of his lord he was fain to requite
in after days; and to Eadgils he proved
friend to the friendless, and forces sent
over the sea to the son of Ohtere,
weapons and warriors: well repaid he
those care-paths cold when the king he slew.
Thus safe through struggles the son of Ecgtheow
had passed a plenty, through perils dire,
with daring deeds, till this day was come

that doomed him now with the dragon to strive.
With comrades eleven the lord of Geats
swollen in rage went seeking the dragon.
He had heard whence all the harm arose
and the killing of clansmen; that cup of price
on the lap of the lord had been laid by the finder.
In the throng was this one thirteenth man,
starter of all the strife and ill,
care-laden captive; cringing thence
forced and reluctant, he led them on
till he came in ken of that cavern-hall,
the barrow delved near billowy surges,
flood of ocean. Within 'twas full
of wire-gold and jewels; a jealous warden,
warrior trusty, the treasures held,
lurked in his lair. Not light the task
of entrance for any of earth-born men!
Sat on the headland the hero king,
spake words of hail to his hearth-companions,
gold-friend of Geats. All gloomy his soul,
wavering, death-bound. Wyrd full nigh
stood ready to greet the gray-haired man,
to seize his soul-hoard, sunder apart
life and body. Not long would be
the warrior's spirit enwound with flesh.
Beowulf spake, the bairn of Ecgtheow:
"Through store of struggles I strove in youth,
mighty feuds; I mind them all.
I was seven years old when the sovran of rings,
friend-of-his-folk, from my father took me,
had me, and held me, Hrethel the king,
with food and fee, faithful in kinship.
Ne'er, while I lived there, he loathlier found me,
bairn in the burg, than his birthright sons,
Herebeald and Haethcyn and Hygelac mine.
For the eldest of these, by unmeet chance,
by kinsman's deed, was the death-bed strewn,
when Haethcyn killed him with horny bow,
his own dear liege laid low with an arrow,
missed the mark and his mate shot down,

one brother the other, with bloody shaft.
A feeless fight, and a fearful sin,
horror to Hrethel; yet, hard as it was,
unavenged must the atheling die!
Too awful it is for an aged man
to bide and bear, that his bairn so young
rides on the gallows. A rime he makes,
sorrow-song for his son there hanging
as rapture of ravens; no rescue now
can come from the old, disabled man!
Still is he minded, as morning breaks,
of the heir gone elsewhere; another he hopes not
he will bide to see his burg within
as ward for his wealth, now the one has found
doom of death that the deed incurred.
Forlorn he looks on the lodge of his son,
wine-hall waste and wind-swept chambers
reft of revel. The rider sleepeth,
the hero, far-hidden; no harp resounds,
in the courts no wassail, as once was heard.

33

"Then he goes to his chamber, a grief-song chants
alone for his lost. Too large all seems,
homestead and house. So the helmet-of-Weders
hid in his heart for Herebeald
waves of woe. No way could he take
to avenge on the slayer slaughter so foul;
nor e'en could he harass that hero at all
with loathing deed, though he loved him not.
And so for the sorrow his soul endured,
men's gladness he gave up and God's light chose.
Lands and cities he left his sons
(as the wealthy do) when he went from earth.
There was strife and struggle 'twixt Swede and Geat
o'er the width of waters; war arose,

hard battle-horror, when Hrethel died,
and Ongentheow's offspring grew
strife-keen, bold, nor brooked o'er the seas
pact of peace, but pushed their hosts
to harass in hatred by Hreosnabeorh.
Men of my folk for that feud had vengeance,
for woeful war ('tis widely known),
though one of them bought it with blood of his heart,
a bargain hard: for Haethcyn proved
fatal that fray, for the first-of-Geats.
At morn, I heard, was the murderer killed
by kinsman for kinsman, with clash of sword,
when Ongentheow met Eofor there.
Wide split the war-helm: wan he fell,
hoary Scylfing; the hand that smote him
of feud was mindful, nor flinched from the death-blow.
"For all that he gave me, my gleaming sword
repaid him at war—such power I wielded—
for lordly treasure: with land he entrusted me,
homestead and house. He had no need
from Swedish realm, or from Spear-Dane folk,
or from men of the Gifths, to get him help,
some warrior worse for wage to buy!
Ever I fought in the front of all,
sole to the fore; and so shall I fight
while I bide in life and this blade shall last
that early and late hath loyal proved
since for my doughtiness Daeghrefn fell,
slain by my hand, the Hugas' champion.
Nor fared he thence to the Frisian king
with the booty back, and breast-adornments;
but, slain in struggle, that standard-bearer
fell, atheling brave. Not with blade was he slain,
but his bones were broken by brawny gripe,
his heart-waves stilled. The sword-edge now,
hard blade and my hand, for the hoard shall strive."
Beowulf spake, and a battle-vow made
his last of all: "I have lived through many
wars in my youth; now once again,
old folk-defender, feud will I seek,

do doughty deeds, if the dark destroyer
forth from his cavern come to fight me!"
Then hailed he the helmeted heroes all,
for the last time greeting his liegemen dear,
comrades of war: "I should carry no weapon,
no sword to the serpent, if sure I knew
how, with such enemy, else my vows
I could gain as I did in Grendel's day.
But fire in this fight I must fear me now,
and poisonous breath; so I bring with me
breastplate and board. From the barrow's keeper
no footbreadth flee I. One fight shall end
our war by the wall, as Wyrd allots,
all mankind's master. My mood is bold
but forbears to boast o'er this battling-flyer.
Now abide by the barrow, ye breastplate-mailed,
ye heroes in harness, which of us twain
better from battle-rush bear his wounds.
Wait ye the finish. The fight is not yours,
nor meet for any but me alone
to measure might with this monster here
and play the hero. Hardily I
shall win that wealth, or war shall seize,
cruel killing, your king and lord!"
Up stood then with shield the sturdy champion,
stayed by the strength of his single manhood,
and hardy 'neath helmet his harness bore
under cleft of the cliffs: no coward's path!
Soon spied by the wall that warrior chief,
survivor of many a victory-field
where foemen fought with furious clashings,
an arch of stone; and within, a stream
that broke from the barrow. The brooklet's wave
was hot with fire. The hoard that way
he never could hope unharmed to near,
or endure those deeps, for the dragon's flame.
Then let from his breast, for he burst with rage,
the Weder-Geat prince a word outgo;
stormed the stark-heart; stern went ringing
and clear his cry 'neath the cliff-rocks gray.

The hoard-guard heard a human voice;
his rage was enkindled. No respite now
for pact of peace! The poison-breath
of that foul worm first came forth from the cave,
hot reek-of-fight: the rocks resounded.
Stout by the stone-way his shield he raised,
lord of the Geats, against the loathed-one;
while with courage keen that coiled foe
came seeking strife. The sturdy king
had drawn his sword, not dull of edge,
heirloom old; and each of the two
felt fear of his foe, though fierce their mood.
Stoutly stood with his shield high-raised
the warrior king, as the worm now coiled
together amain: the mailed-one waited.
Now, spire by spire, fast sped and glided
that blazing serpent. The shield protected,
soul and body a shorter while
for the hero-king than his heart desired,
could his will have wielded the welcome respite
but once in his life! But Wyrd denied it,
and victory's honors. His arm he lifted
lord of the Geats, the grim foe smote
with atheling's heirloom. Its edge was turned
brown blade, on the bone, and bit more feebly
than its noble master had need of then
in his baleful stress. Then the barrow's keeper
waxed full wild for that weighty blow,
cast deadly flames; wide drove and far
those vicious fires. No victor's glory
the Geats' lord boasted; his brand had failed,
naked in battle, as never it should,
excellent iron! 'Twas no easy path
that Ecgtheow's honored heir must tread
over the plain to the place of the foe;
for against his will he must win a home
elsewhere far, as must all men, leaving
this lapsing life! Not long it was
ere those champions grimly closed again.
The hoard-guard was heartened; high heaved his breast

once more; and by peril was pressed again,
enfolded in flames, the folk-commander!
Nor yet about him his band of comrades,
sons of athelings, armed stood
with warlike front: to the woods they bent them,
their lives to save. But the soul of one
with care was cumbered. Kinship true
can never be marred in a noble mind!

34

Wiglaf his name was, Weohstan's son,
linden-thane loved, the lord of Scylfings,
Aelfhere's kinsman. His king he now saw
with heat under helmet hard oppressed.
He minded the prizes his prince had given him,
wealthy seat of the Waegmunding line,
and folk-rights that his father owned.
Not long he lingered. The linden yellow,
his shield, he seized; the old sword he drew:
as heirloom of Eanmund earth-dwellers knew it,
who was slain by the sword-edge, son of Ohtere,
friendless exile, erst in fray
killed by Weohstan, who won for his kin
brown-bright helmet, breastplate ringed,
old sword of Eotens, Onela's gift,
weeds of war of the warrior-thane,
battle-gear brave: though a brother's child
had been felled, the feud was unfelt by Onela.
For winters this war-gear Weohstan kept,
breastplate and board, till his bairn had grown
earlship to earn as the old sire did:
then he gave him, mid Geats, the gear of battle,
portion huge, when he passed from life,
fared aged forth. For the first time now
with his leader-lord the liegeman young

was bidden to share the shock of battle.
Neither softened his soul, nor the sire's bequest
weakened in war. So the worm found out
when once in fight the foes had met!
Wiglaf spake, and his words were sage;
sad in spirit, he said to his comrades:
"I remember the time, when mead we took,
what promise we made to this prince of ours
in the banquet-hall, to our breaker-of-rings,
for gear of combat to give him requital,
for hard-sword and helmet, if hap should bring
stress of this sort! Himself who chose us
from all his army to aid him now,
urged us to glory, and gave these treasures,
because he counted us keen with the spear
and hardy 'neath helm, though this hero-work
our leader hoped unhelped and alone
to finish for us—folk-defender
who hath got him glory greater than all men
for daring deeds! Now the day is come
that our noble master has need of the might
of warriors stout. Let us stride along
the hero to help while the heat is about him
glowing and grim! For God is my witness
I am far more fain the fire should seize
along with my lord these limbs of mine!
Unsuiting it seems our shields to bear
homeward hence, save here we essay
to fell the foe and defend the life
of the Weders' lord. I wot 'twere shame
on the law of our land if alone the king
out of Geatish warriors woe endured
and sank in the struggle! My sword and helmet,
breastplate and board, for us both shall serve!"
Through slaughter-reek strode he to succor his chieftain,
his battle-helm bore, and brief words spake:
"Beowulf dearest, do all bravely,
as in youthful days of yore thou vowedst
that while life should last thou wouldst let no wise

thy glory droop! Now, great in deeds,
atheling steadfast, with all thy strength
shield thy life! I will stand to help thee."
At the words the worm came once again,
murderous monster mad with rage,
with fire-billows flaming, its foes to seek,
the hated men. In heat-waves burned
that board to the boss, and the breastplate failed
to shelter at all the spear-thane young.
Yet quickly under his kinsman's shield
went eager the earl, since his own was now
all burned by the blaze. The bold king again
had mind of his glory: with might his glaive
was driven into the dragon's head—
blow nerved by hate. But Naegling was shivered,
broken in battle was Beowulf's sword,
old and gray. 'Twas granted him not
that ever the edge of iron at all
could help him at strife: too strong was his hand,
so the tale is told, and he tried too far
with strength of stroke all swords he wielded,
though sturdy their steel: they steaded him nought.
Then for the third time thought on its feud
that folk-destroyer, fire-dread dragon,
and rushed on the hero, where room allowed,
battle-grim, burning; its bitter teeth
closed on his neck, and covered him
with waves of blood from his breast that welled.

35

'Twas now, men say, in his sovran's need
that the earl made known his noble strain,
craft and keenness and courage enduring.
Heedless of harm, though his hand was burned,
hardy-hearted, he helped his kinsman.

A little lower the loathsome beast
he smote with sword; his steel drove in
bright and burnished; that blaze began
to lose and lessen. At last the king
wielded his wits again, war-knife drew,
a biting blade by his breastplate hanging,
and the Weders'-helm smote that worm asunder,
felled the foe, flung forth its life.
So had they killed it, kinsmen both,
athelings twain: thus an earl should be
in danger's day! Of deeds of valor
this conqueror's-hour of the king was last,
of his work in the world. The wound began,
which that dragon-of-earth had erst inflicted,
to swell and smart; and soon he found
in his breast was boiling, baleful and deep,
pain of poison. The prince walked on,
wise in his thought, to the wall of rock;
then sat, and stared at the structure of giants,
where arch of stone and steadfast column
upheld forever that hall in earth.
Yet here must the hand of the henchman peerless
lave with water his winsome lord,
the king and conqueror covered with blood,
with struggle spent, and unspan his helmet.
Beowulf spake in spite of his hurt,
his mortal wound; full well he knew
his portion now was past and gone
of earthly bliss, and all had fled
of his file of days, and death was near:
"I would fain bestow on son of mine
this gear of war, were given me now
that any heir should after me come
of my proper blood. This people I ruled
fifty winters. No folk-king was there,
none at all, of the neighboring clans
who war would wage me with 'warriors'-friends'
and threat me with horrors. At home I bided
what fate might come, and I cared for mine own;

feuds I sought not, nor falsely swore
ever on oath. For all these things,
though fatally wounded, fain am I!
From the Ruler-of-Man no wrath shall seize me,
when life from my frame must flee away,
for killing of kinsmen! Now quickly go
and gaze on that hoard 'neath the hoary rock,
Wiglaf loved, now the worm lies low,
sleeps, heart-sore, of his spoil bereaved.
And fare in haste. I would fain behold
the gorgeous heirlooms, golden store,
have joy in the jewels and gems, lay down
softlier for sight of this splendid hoard
my life and the lordship I long have held."

36

I have heard that swiftly the son of Weohstan
at wish and word of his wounded king—
war-sick warrior—woven mail-coat,
battle-sark, bore 'neath the barrow's roof.
Then the clansman keen, of conquest proud,
passing the seat, saw store of jewels
and glistening gold the ground along;
by the wall were marvels, and many a vessel
in the den of the dragon, the dawn-flier old:
unburnished bowls of bygone men
reft of richness; rusty helms
of the olden age; and arm-rings many
wondrously woven. Such wealth of gold,
booty from barrow, can burden with pride
each human wight: let him hide it who will!
His glance too fell on a gold-wove banner
high o'er the hoard, of handiwork noblest,
brilliantly broidered; so bright its gleam,
all the earth-floor he easily saw
and viewed all these vessels. No vestige now

was seen of the serpent: the sword had ta'en him.
Then, I heard, the hill of its hoard was reft,
old work of giants, by one alone;
he burdened his bosom with beakers and plate
at his own good will, and the ensign took,
brightest of beacons. The blade of his lord—
its edge was iron—had injured deep
one that guarded the golden hoard
many a year and its murder-fire
spread hot round the barrow in horror-billows
at midnight hour, till it met its doom.
Hasted the herald, the hoard so spurred him
his track to retrace; he was troubled by doubt,
high-souled hero, if haply he'd find
alive, where he left him, the lord of Weders,
weakening fast by the wall of the cave.
So he carried the load. His lord and king
he found all bleeding, famous chief
at the lapse of life. The liegeman again
plashed him with water, till point of word
broke through the breast-hoard. Beowulf spake,
sage and sad, as he stared at the gold.
"For the gold and treasure, to God my thanks,
to the Wielder-of-Wonders, with words I say,
for what I behold, to Heaven's Lord,
for the grace that I give such gifts to my folk
or ever the day of my death be run!
Now I've bartered here for booty of treasure
the last of my life, so look ye well
to the needs of my land! No longer I tarry.
A barrow bid ye the battle-fanned raise
for my ashes. 'Twill shine by the shore of the flood,
to folk of mine memorial fair
on Hrones Headland high uplifted,
that ocean-wanderers oft may hail
Beowulf's Barrow, as back from far
they drive their keels o'er the darkling wave."
From his neck he unclasped the collar of gold,
valorous king, to his vassal gave it

with bright-gold helmet, breastplate, and ring,
to the youthful thane: bade him use them in joy.
"Thou art end and remnant of all our race
the Waegmunding name. For Wyrd hath swept them,
all my line, to the land of doom,
earls in their glory: I after them go."
This word was the last which the wise old man
harbored in heart ere hot death-waves
of balefire he chose. From his bosom fled
his soul to seek the saints' reward.

37

It was heavy hap for that hero young
on his lord beloved to look and find him
lying on earth with life at end,
sorrowful sight. But the slayer too,
awful earth-dragon, empty of breath,
lay felled in fight, nor, fain of its treasure,
could the writhing monster rule it more.
For edges of iron had ended its days,
hard and battle-sharp, hammers' leaving;
and that flier-afar had fallen to ground
hushed by its hurt, its hoard all near,
no longer lusty aloft to whirl
at midnight, making its merriment seen,
proud of its prizes: prone it sank
by the handiwork of the hero-king.
Forsooth among folk but few achieve—
though sturdy and strong, as stories tell me,
and never so daring in deed of valor—
the perilous breath of a poison-foe
to brave, and to rush on the ring-board hall,
whenever his watch the warden keeps
bold in the barrow. Beowulf paid
the price of death for that precious hoard;
and each of the foes had found the end

of this fleeting life. Befell erelong
that the laggards in war the wood had left,
trothbreakers, cowards, ten together,
fearing before to flourish a spear
in the sore distress of their sovran lord.
Now in their shame their shields they carried,
armor of fight, where the old man lay;
and they gazed on Wiglaf. Wearied he sat
at his sovran's shoulder, shieldsman good,
to wake him with water. Nowise it availed.
Though well he wished it, in world no more
could he barrier life for that leader-of-battles
nor baffle the will of all-wielding God.
Doom of the Lord was law o'er the deeds
of every man, as it is today.
Grim was the answer, easy to get,
from the youth for those that had yielded to fear!
Wiglaf spake, the son of Weohstan—
mournful he looked on those men unloved—
"Who sooth will speak, can say indeed
that the ruler who gave you golden rings
and the harness of war in which ye stand—
for he at ale-bench often-times
bestowed on hall-folk helm and breastplate,
lord to liegemen, the likeliest gear
which near or far he could find to give—
threw away and wasted these weeds of battle,
on men who failed when the foemen came!
Not at all could the king of his comrades-in-arms
venture to vaunt, though the Victory-Wielder,
God, gave him grace that he got revenge
sole with his sword in stress and need.
To rescue his life, 'twas little that I
could serve him in struggle; yet shift I made
(hopeless it seemed) to help my kinsman.
Its strength ever waned, when with weapon I struck
that fatal foe, and the fire less strongly
flowed from its head. Too few the heroes
in throe of contest that thronged to our king!
Now gift of treasure and girding of sword,

joy of the house and home-delight
shall fail your folk; his freehold-land
every clansman within your kin
shall lose and leave, when lords high-born
hear afar of that flight of yours,
a fameless deed. Yea, death is better
for liegemen all than a life of shame!"

38

That battle-toil bade he at burg to announce,
at the fort on the cliff, where, full of sorrow,
all the morning earls had sat,
daring shieldsmen, in doubt of twain:
would they wail as dead, or welcome home,
their lord beloved? Little kept back
of the tidings new, but told them all,
the herald that up the headland rode.
"Now the willing-giver to Weder folk
in death-bed lies; the Lord of Geats
on the slaughter-bed sleeps by the serpent's deed!
And beside him is stretched that slayer-of-men
with knife-wounds sick: no sword availed
on the awesome thing in any wise
to work a wound. There Wiglaf sitteth,
Weohstan's bairn, by Beowulf's side,
the living earl by the other dead,
and heavy of heart a head-watch keeps
o'er friend and foe. Now our folk may look
for waging of war when once unhidden
to Frisian and Frank the fall of the king
is spread afar. The strife began
when hot on the Hugas Hygelac fell
and fared with his fleet to the Frisian land.
Him there the Hetwaras humbled in war,
plied with such prowess their power o'erwhelming
that the bold-in-battle bowed beneath it

and fell in fight. To his friends no wise
could that earl give treasure! And ever since
the Merowings' favor has failed us wholly.
Nor aught expect I of peace and faith
from Swedish folk. 'Twas spread afar
how Ongentheow reft at Ravenswood
Haethcyn Hrethling of hope and life,
when the folk of Geats for the first time sought
in wanton pride the Warlike-Scylfings.
Soon the sage old sire of Ohtere,
ancient and awful, gave answering blow;
the sea-king he slew, and his spouse redeemed,
his good wife rescued, though robbed of her gold,
mother of Ohtere and Onela.
Then he followed his foes, who fled before him
sore beset and stole their way,
bereft of a ruler, to Ravenswood.

With his host he besieged there what swords had left,
the weary and wounded; woes he threatened
the whole night through to that hard-pressed throng:
some with the morrow his sword should kill,
some should go to the gallows-tree
for rapture of ravens. But rescue came
with dawn of day for those desperate men
when they heard the horn of Hygelac sound,
tones of his trumpet; the trusty king
had followed their trail with faithful band.

39

"The bloody swath of Swedes and Geats
and the storm of their strife, were seen afar,
how folk against folk the fight had wakened.
The ancient king with his atheling band
sought his citadel, sorrowing much:
Ongentheow earl went up to his burg.

He had tested Hygelac's hardihood,
the proud one's prowess, would prove it no longer,
defied no more those fighting-wanderers
nor hoped from the seamen to save his hoard,
his bairn and his bride: so he bent him again,
old, to his earth-walls. Yet after him came
with slaughter for Swedes the standards of Hygelac
o'er peaceful plains in pride advancing,
till Hrethelings fought in the fenced town.
Then Ongentheow with edge of sword,
the hoary-bearded, was held at bay,
and the folk-king there was forced to suffer
Eofor's anger. In ire, at the king
Wulf Wonreding with weapon struck;
and the chieftain's blood, for that blow, in streams
flowed 'neath his hair. No fear felt he,
stout old Scylfing, but straightway repaid
in better bargain that bitter stroke
and faced his foe with fell intent.
Nor swift enough was the son of Wonred
answer to render the aged chief;
too soon on his head the helm was cloven;
blood-bedecked he bowed to earth,
and fell adown; not doomed was he yet,
and well he waxed, though the wound was sore.
Then the hardy Hygelac-thane,
when his brother fell, with broad brand smote,
giants' sword crashing through giants'-helm
across the shield-wall: sank the king,
his folk's old herdsman, fatally hurt.
There were many to bind the brother's wounds
and lift him, fast as fate allowed
his people to wield the place-of-war.
But Eofor took from Ongentheow,
earl from other, the iron-breastplate,
hard sword hilted, and helmet too,
and the hoar-chief's harness to Hygelac carried,
who took the trappings, and truly promised
rich fee 'mid folk, and fulfilled it so.
For that grim strife gave the Geatish lord,

Hrethel's offspring, when home he came,
to Eofor and Wulf a wealth of treasure,
Each of them had a hundred thousand
in land and linked rings; nor at less price reckoned
mid-earth men such mighty deeds!
And to Eofor he gave his only daughter
in pledge of grace, the pride of his home.

"Such is the feud, the foeman's rage,
death-hate of men: so I deem it sure
that the Swedish folk will seek us home
for this fall of their friends, the fighting-Scylfings,
when once they learn that our warrior leader
lifeless lies, who land and hoard
ever defended from all his foes,
furthered his folk's weal, finished his course
a hardy hero. Now haste is best,
that we go to gaze on our Geatish lord,
and bear the bountiful breaker-of-rings
to the funeral pyre. No fragments merely
shall burn with the warrior. Wealth of jewels,
gold untold and gained in terror,
treasure at last with his life obtained,
all of that booty the brands shall take,
fire shall eat it. No earl must carry
memorial jewel. No maiden fair
shall wreathe her neck with noble ring:
nay, sad in spirit and shorn of her gold,
oft shall she pass o'er paths of exile
now our lord all laughter has laid aside,
all mirth and revel. Many a spear
morning-cold shall be clasped amain,
lifted aloft; nor shall lilt of harp
those warriors wake; but the wan-hued raven,
fain o'er the fallen, his feast shall praise
and boast to the eagle how bravely he ate
when he and the wolf were wasting the slain."

So he told his sorrowful tidings,
and little he lied, the loyal man

of word or of work. The warriors rose;
sad, they climbed to the Cliff-of-Eagles,
went, welling with tears, the wonder to view.
Found on the sand there, stretched at rest,
their lifeless lord, who had lavished rings
of old upon them. Ending-day
had dawned on the doughty one; death had seized
in woeful slaughter the Weders' king.
There saw they, besides, the strangest being,
loathsome, lying their leader near,
prone on the field. The fiery dragon,
fearful fiend, with flame was scorched.
Reckoned by feet, it was fifty measures
in length as it lay. Aloft erewhile
it had revelled by night, and anon come back,
seeking its den; now in death's sure clutch
it had come to the end of its earth-hall joys.
By it there stood the stoups and jars;
dishes lay there, and dear-decked swords
eaten with rust, as, on earth's lap resting,
a thousand winters they waited there.
For all that heritage huge, that gold
of bygone men, was bound by a spell,
so the treasure-hall could be touched by none
of human kind—save that Heaven's King,
God himself, might give whom he would,
Helper of Heroes, the hoard to open—
even such a man as seemed to him meet.

40

A perilous path, it proved, he trod
who heinously hid, that hall within,
wealth under wall! Its watcher had killed
one of a few, and the feud was avenged
in woeful fashion. Wondrous seems it,
what manner a man of might and valor
oft ends his life, when the earl no longer

in mead-hall may live with loving friends.
So Beowulf, when that barrow's warden
he sought, and the struggle; himself knew not
in what wise he should wend from the world at last.
For princes potent, who placed the gold,
with a curse to doomsday covered it deep,
so that marked with sin the man should be,
hedged with horrors, in hell-bonds fast,
racked with plagues, who should rob their hoard.
Yet no greed for gold, but the grace of heaven,
ever the king had kept in view.
Wiglaf spake, the son of Weohstan:
"At the mandate of one, oft warriors many
sorrow must suffer; and so must we.
The people's-shepherd showed not aught
of care for our counsel, king beloved!
That guardian of gold he should grapple not, urged we,
but let him lie where he long had been
in his earth-hall waiting the end of the world,
the hest of heaven. This hoard is ours
but grievously gotten; too grim the fate
which thither carried our king and lord.
I was within there, and all I viewed,
the chambered treasure, when chance allowed me
(and my path was made in no pleasant wise)
under the earth-wall. Eager, I seized
such heap from the hoard as hands could bear
and hurriedly carried it hither back
to my liege and lord. Alive was he still,
still wielding his wits. The wise old man
spake much in his sorrow, and sent you greetings
and bade that ye build, when he breathed no more,
on the place of his balefire a barrow high,
memorial mighty. Of men was he
worthiest warrior wide earth o'er
the while he had joy of his jewels and burg.
Let us set out in haste now, the second time
to see and search this store of treasure,
these wall-hid wonders—the way I show you—
where, gathered near, ye may gaze your fill

at broad-gold and rings. Let the bier, soon made,
be all in order when out we come,
our king and captain to carry thither—
man beloved—where long he shall bide
safe in the shelter of sovran God."
Then the bairn of Weohstan bade command,
hardy chief, to heroes many
that owned their homesteads, hither to bring
firewood from far—o'er the folk they ruled—
for the famed-one's funeral. "Fire shall devour
and wan flames feed on the fearless warrior
who oft stood stout in the iron-shower,
when, sped from the string, a storm of arrows
shot o'er the shield-wall: the shaft held firm,
featly feathered, followed the barb."
And now the sage young son of Weohstan
seven chose of the chieftain's thanes,
the best he found that band within,
and went with these warriors, one of eight,
under hostile roof. In hand one bore
a lighted torch and led the way.
No lots they cast for keeping the hoard
when once the warriors saw it in hall,
altogether without a guardian,
lying there lost. And little they mourned
when they had hastily haled it out,
dear-bought treasure! The dragon they cast,
the worm, o'er the wall for the wave to take,
and surges swallowed that shepherd of gems.
Then the woven gold on a wain was laden—
countless quite!—and the king was borne,
hoary hero, to Hrones-Ness.

41

Then fashioned for him the folk of Geats
firm on the earth a funeral-pile,

and hung it with helmets and harness of war
and breastplates bright, as the boon he asked;
and they laid amid it the mighty chieftain,
heroes mourning their master dear.
Then on the hill that hugest of balefires
the warriors wakened. Wood-smoke rose
black over blaze, and blent was the roar
of flame with weeping (the wind was still),
till the fire had broken the frame of bones,
hot at the heart. In heavy mood
their misery moaned they, their master's death.
Wailing her woe, the widow old,
her hair upbound, for Beowulf's death
sung in her sorrow, and said full oft
she dreaded the doleful days to come,
deaths enow, and doom of battle,
and shame. The smoke by the sky was devoured.
The folk of the Weders fashioned there
on the headland a barrow broad and high,
by ocean-farers far descried:
in ten days' time their toil had raised it,
the battle-brave's beacon. Round brands of the pyre
a wall they built, the worthiest ever
that wit could prompt in their wisest men.
They placed in the barrow that precious booty,
the rounds and the rings they had reft erewhile,
hardy heroes, from hoard in cave,
trusting the ground with treasure of earls,
gold in the earth, where ever it lies
useless to men as of yore it was.
Then about that barrow the battle-keen rode,
atheling-born, a band of twelve,
lament to make, to mourn their king,
chant their dirge, and their chieftain honor.
They praised his earlship, his acts of prowess
worthily witnessed: and well it is
that men their master-friend mightily laud,
heartily love, when hence he goes
from life in the body forlorn away.

Thus made their mourning the men of Geatland,
for their hero's passing his hearth-companions:
quoth that of all the kings of earth,
of men he was mildest and most beloved,
to his kin the kindest, keenest for praise.

BEOWULF

PROSE

Prelude

Lo! We have heard tell of the might in days of old of the Spear-Dane's[1] folk-kings, how deeds of prowess were wrought by the athelings. Oft Scyld Scefing reft away their mead-benches from the throngs of his foes, from many a people. Fear came of the earl, after he was found at the first in his need.[2] Redress he won for that, waxed under the clouds, throve in his glories, till of them that dwelt nigh him over the whale-road, each must obey him, and pay him tribute. That was a good king!

To him in after time a son was born, young in his courts, whom God sent for a help to the people, for he saw the dire need they had suffered long time till then through lack of a leader; for this the Lord of Life, the King of Glory, gave him honor in the world. Renowned was Beowulf;[3] the fame of the son of Scyld spread wide in the Scedelands.[4] In such wise worthily among his father's friends by goodly gifts of gold must a man in his youth so prevail that in old age, when war shall come, willing comrades may cleave to their lord and do him service; among every people a man shall thrive by deeds of praise.

Then, at the hour of his fate, in fulness of valor, Scyld went his way. They bare him forth to the sea-flood, his own close comrades, as he had himself bidden them, the while he, the Scyldings' friend,

---

[1]The Danes, in allusion to their valor, wide dominions, or their ruling house (the Scyldings, or descendants of Scyld), are called Spear-Danes, Ring- or Armor-Danes, Bright-Danes; East-, West-, South-, and North-Danes; Scyldings, Victor-Scyldings, etc. They are also called Hrethmen and Ingwines. The Geats similarly are called Weders, or Weder-Geats, Sea- or War-Geats, and the Swedes are called Scylfings.

[2]Scyld drifted to the shores of the Danes, as a helpless infant in a boat which bare also much treasure; compare the later reference, p. 94 ("Truly with no less," etc.).

[3]The son of Scyld, not Beowulf the Geat, the hero of the poem.

[4]Also Scedenig; part of the Danish kingdom, situated according to a generally accepted view at the extreme southern part of the Scandinavian peninsula; here used for the whole kingdom.

the land's dear lord, long time held sway by his word. There at the haven stood the ringed prow, the atheling's ship, gleaming and eager to start. They laid him down then, their lord beloved, the ring-giver, in the ship's bosom, placed the mighty one at the mast.

Much treasure was there, trappings of price from far-off lands. Never heard I of keel fitted out more bravely with weapons of war and weeds of battle, with bills and with burnies. A heap of jewels lay in his bosom that must needs fare far with him into the grip of the flood. Truly with no less gift-offerings and folk-treasures did they in this wise dispose him than they that at his birth sent him forth alone on the waves, being but a child. Thereto they set for him a golden standard high overhead, let the wave bear him, gave him to the deep. Sorrow of soul was theirs and mood of mourning. Men dwelling in halls, heroes under heaven, cannot in truth say who came by that lading.

1

For long thereafter in the walled towns was Beowulf, the loved folk-king of the Scyldings, known to fame among the peoples (his father had gone elsewhere, the prince from his own), till in time was born to him the great Healfdene, who, whilst he lived, ruled the Scyldings in kindness, the ancient one, fierce in battle.

To him, leader of battle-hosts, four children were born into the world, which were, told in order, Heorogar, and Hrothgar, and Halga the Brave, while Sigeneow, as I have heard say, was Sæwela's queen,[1] the valorous Scylfing's beloved bed-sharer. Fortune in battle was given then to Hrothgar and fame in war, so that, by the time the youth grew of age, his dear kinsfolk, a great following of young warriors, obeyed him gladly.

It came to his mind to bid men build him a hall-dwelling, a mead-house, greater than children of men had ever heard of, and that there

---

[1]This rendering follows Kluge's reconstruction of an illegible passage in the manuscript, based on a mention in the "Hrolf Saga" of a daughter of Healfdene and her husband. Grein's reconstruction, hitherto adopted in default of a better, assumes a daughter Elan, married to Ongentheow. Trautmann has suggested the names Yrde and Onela.

within it he would part to young and old what God had given him,
save the people's land and the lives of men. Then, as I heard, on
many a kindred far and wide through the mid-earth[1] was the task
laid of making fair the folk-hall. Speedily it befell him in time among
men that it was in every wise ready, the greatest of hall-houses, and
he made for it, who far and wide held sway by his word, the name
of Heorot. He belied not his pledge and dealt out rings and treasure
at the feast. The hall rose lofty and broad-gabled. Warring surges it
awaited of loathly flame,[2] nor was it long before deadly hate must
awaken through the murderous strife of son and father-in-law.

Then the demon fell, that dwelt in darkness, scarce for a space
endured that he should hear each day rejoicing loud in the hall; there
was sound of the harp there and clear song of the gleeman. One
spake that knew[3] how to tell of man's first making of old, said that
the Almighty framed the world, the plain bright in beauty which
the waters encircle, and, glorying in His handiwork, set the sun and
moon to lighten the earth-dwellers, and decked the corners of the
earth with boughs and leaves, and gave life to every kind of crea-
ture that walks alive. So the warriors lived in joy and plenty, till one,
a fiend of hell, began to do evil. The grim demon, the fell prowler
about the borders of the homes of men, who held the moors, the fens,
and the fastnesses, was called Grendel. In the domain of the giant-
race, Cain, the man reft of joy, dwelt for a time, after the Creator
had doomed him. On his posterity the Eternal Lord took vengeance
for the murder, in that he slew Abel. God took no joy in that feud,
but banished him, for his deed, far from mankind. By him were the
wanton ones all begotten, the eotens[4] and elves and monsters of the
deep, the giants also who strove long against God—for that He repaid
them in due requital.

---

[1]The earth, according to Teutonic mythology, was surrounded by the sea.

[2]The poet refers to the final destruction of the hall, not described in the poem.
The hatred and strife referred to is that between Hrothgar and Ingeld: see foot-
note [1] on p. 136 ("Therefore it may ill please," etc.).

[3]A Christian interpolation, inappropriate if meant to give the burden of the
gleeman's song. The poem elsewhere usually discriminates the fact that the
period of the story is heathen. The attribution to Grendel below of a descent
from Cain is a notable Christian addition.

[4]The giants of Teutonic mythology. The Anglo-Saxon word is retained as char-
acteristic, and because of the use, just below, of *gigantas*, giants, a borrowing
from the Latin.

2

Then went Grendel, when night had come, to spy about the high house and see how the Ring-Danes had left it after the beer-drinking. There he found the company of athelings sleeping after the feast; sorrow they knew not, or the evil haps of men. The baneful wight, grim and greedy, fierce and pitiless, was soon alert, and took, where they rested, thirty thanes. Thence fared he back homeward, boastfully exultant over his spoil, and sought his abiding-places with that glut of slaughter.

Thereupon at dawn, with break of day, plain enough to the warriors was Grendel's might in strife. Then was weeping upraised after all their glad feasting, a great cry at dawn. When they had seen the track of the loathly one, the woeful demon, the prince renowned, the atheling passing good, sat joyless, under went heaviness of grief, suffered sorrow for his thanes; too sore was that trouble, too hateful and lingering. Nor was it longer than after one night that Grendel again wrought murderous destruction still more grievous, nor reeked of the violence and evil—too fixed was he in them. It was easy then finding one who sought a place of rest for himself farther away, a bed apart from the buildings, now that the hate of that thane of hell had been shown and truly declared by a clear token; he kept himself farther away from then on, and in some safer place, that might escape the demon.

Thus had Grendel mastery and warred against the right, he alone against all, till the fairest of houses stood idle. A great while it was, twelve winters' season, that the friend of the Scyldings endured this trouble, every woe, the utmost of sorrow. In due course thereafter it became known openly to the children of men through songs sorrowfully, that Grendel had striven for a time against Hrothgar, waged for many half-years a ruthless war, ceaseless strife, evil, and violence, nor would in peaceful wise lift the deadly doom from any man of the might of the Danes, nor durst any even among the worshipful ones look for better fortune at the slayer's hands. The grisly monster, the dark death-shadow, rested not in pursuit of young and old, lay in wait and made ambush. Night after night he held the misty moors; men know not whither the creatures of hell will walk on their rounds.

In this wise, often, the enemy of mankind, the lonely one terrible, wrought many an outrage, deeds that shamed them hard to bear.

On dark nights he stayed in Heorot, the hall brave with gold, yet he might not touch the gift-stool—its treasures he scorned—nor knew he desire for it.

That was a great grief and sorrow of heart to the friend of the Scyldings. Many a one strong in council oft sat deliberating; counsel they devised what with bold hearts it were best to do against the terror descending unforeseen. Sometimes they vowed offerings in their temples of idols, besought with words of prayer that the slayer of demons would find relief for the people's sorrow. Such was their custom, the trust of the heathen; the thoughts of their breasts were intent on hell, the Creator they knew not—knew not the judge of men's deeds, the Lord God, nor truly knew they how to praise the Guardian of the Heavens, the King of Glory. Woe shall be his who needs must through his fierce frowardness thrust down his soul into the bosom of the fire, look for no comfort, in no wise return; well shall it be for him that may, after the day of death, seek out the Lord and plead for peace in the Father's bosom.

3

Thus then without ceasing the son of Healfdene brooded his season of sorrow. The wise warrior might not amend his woes; too sore was the strife, the dire distress, greatest of evils of the night, that had come on the people, too hateful and lingering. Of this and Grendel's deeds, the thane of Hygelac,[1] of goodly fame among the Geats, heard tell when from home. Strongest in might of manhood was he in this life's day, noble and powerful. He bade be fitted for himself a good sea-goer, said he would seek out the war-king, the mighty prince over the swan-road, seeing he had need of men. Men deemed wise blamed him no whit for that journey, dear though he was to them. They spurred on the valiant-minded hero, and sought signs for casting his fortune.

He, the worthy one, took to himself picked warriors of the Geat-folk, the boldest he might find. One of fifteen, he set out for the sea-wood. A man skilled in the sea pointed out the landmarks. Time

---

[1]Beowulf the Geat, the hero of the poem. The land of the Geats, the kingdom of Hygelac, is held to have been in the southern part of the Scandinavian peninsula, north of Scedenig (see footnote 4, p. 93, on "Scedelands").

went on, the ship was on the wave, the boat beneath the bluff. The warriors ready went up on the prow. The currents of the sea eddied along the shore. The warsmen bare their bright trappings, war-gear splendrous, into the bosom of the vessel. The men shoved out the well-joined wood on its willing journey. Then went over the billowy sea, sped by the wind, the foamy-necked ship, likest to a bird, till next day at the hour awaited the curved prow had gone so far that the sea-farers might see the land, the shore-cliffs gleam, the broad sea-nesses. Then was the ocean-farer at end of its voyage.

Thereupon the folk of the Weders stepped up quickly on the plain and tied the sea-wood; their sarks rattled, their weeds of war. God they thanked because the wave-paths had proved easy for them. Then from the steep shore, the warden of the Scyldings, whose duty it was to keep watch of the sea-cliffs, saw them bear over the bulwarks their shining shields and gear ready as for battle. He was fretted in his mind's thought with the wish to know what men they were. The thane of Hrothgar went riding, therefore, on his horse to the shore; stoutly he shook the mighty shaft in his hands, asked in words duly considered: "What men are ye having battle-gear, clad in burnies, who thus come leading a deep ship hither over the sea-road, over the waters? I have long been boundary warden, kept watch of the shore, that no foe with a ship's company might work harm in the land of the Danes. No bearers of shields ever undertook to come hither more openly; surely you had not leave from the wagers of war, the consent of the kinsfolk. Never saw I in the world a greater earl or warrior in harness, than is one of you. No lurker at home in the hall is he, with weapons bedight, save his looks and matchless aspect lie. Now must I learn of what blood ye are, ere ye fare further as false spies into the Danes' land. Hear ye now, ye seafaring ones, dwelling afar, my plain thought; it is best most quickly to make known whence ye come."

4

To him the most worshipful one, the leader of the company, spake in answer: "We are of the kin of the Geat-folk and Hygelac's hearth-companions. My father, Ecgtheow by name, the noble high-prince, was known to the peoples. He bided years a many ere he went hoary from his home. Every man of wise mind far and wide remembereth him well. We have come with kind intent to seek thy lord, the son of Healfdene, the people's protector. Be thou good in advising us. We have a weighty errand to the famed lord of the Danes, nor shall any part of it, as I ween, be kept hid. Thou knowest if it be so, as we have truly heard tell, that among the Scyldings a secret foe, I know not what of spoilers, giveth on dark nights proof of hate beyond the know-ing through the terror he worketh, through fell deeds and death-fall. I, therefore, out of largeness of soul may counsel Hrothgar, how he, the wise one and good, may master the foe, if that ever the press of his troubles may know change, solace come after, and the waves of care grow cooler, else he shall suffer this season of sorrow forever, stress of need, so long as in its high place shall stand the fairest of houses."

The warden spake, the fearless retainer, where he sat on his horse: "Of each of these, of words and works, must an able warrior who judgeth well know the difference. I gather that this fellowship is of true thought toward the lord of the Scyldings. Bear forth then your weapons and gear. I shall guide you, and likewise bid my war-thanes keep in due charge from any foe your ship, the newly tarred vessel, on the shore, till that the bent-necked wood bear back the hero beloved, over the sea-streams, to the bounds of the Weders. To a wager of war such as he will it be given to come out unhurt from this bout of bat-tle."

Then went they to him. The ship stayed without moving; the broad-beamed craft rested on its cable at anchor. The graven boars[1] shone over their gold-decked cheek-guards, gleaming and tempered in the fire; grimly warlike of temper, the boar kept his watch. The men hastened on; they went together till they might see, splendid and covered with gold, the timbered house where the king dwelt, that was among earth-dwellers famed beyond all others of halls under heaven—the sheen of it flashed over many lands. Then the bold one in battle showed them the home of brave men where it shone, that they might go to it straightway; he, one from among its warsmen, turned his horse and word spake after: "It is time for me to go. May the Father Almighty through His grace keep you safe in your goings. I will to the sea to keep watch for unfriendly folk."

---

[1]Images of boars serving as crests on their helmets.

5

The street was cobbled; it showed the men the way as they went together. The war-burnie gleamed, hard and hand-linked, the bright-ringed iron sang in their harness, as they then first came faring to the hall in their trappings of terror.

Spent with the sea, they set up their broad shields, their well-hardened bucklers against the wall of the hall, and bowed them to the benches; their burnies and war-gear rang. The spears, the seamen's weapons, stood in one place together with the shafts of ash-wood gray above; the mailed band was well dight with weapons. A proud warrior then asked the warsmen, where they sat, of what kin they were: "Whence bear ye your shields covered with gold, your gray battle-sarks, and helmets grim, your heap of battle-shafts. I am Hrothgar's herald and serving-man. Never saw I, of stranger folk, thus many men of more valiant bearing. I ween in proud daring, not as driven to exile but through greatness of soul, have ye sought Hrothgar."

Him then the proud prince of the Weders, strong in might, answered, and word spake after: "We are Hygelac's table-comrades. Beowulf is my name. I will tell thy lord, the mighty prince, the son of Healfdene, mine errand, if he will grant us, good as he is, to give him greeting."

Wulfgar spake; he was prince of the Wendles; his boldness of heart, his prowess and wisdom were known unto many: "I will ask the mighty prince, the giver of rings, the lord of the Scyldings, friend of the Danes, as thou desirest, concerning thine errand, and quickly make known to thee the answer he of his goodness thinketh to give me."

He turned him then quickly where Hrothgar sat, old and with hair exceeding white, among his band of earls. The valiant one went till he stood at the shoulder[1] of the lord of the Danes, for he knew the ways of men of gentle birth. Wulfgar spake to his gracious lord: "Hither have fared over the ocean-stretches, come from afar, men of the Geats. The warriors name the foremost man among them Beowulf. They pray, my lord, that they may exchange speech with thee. Make thou not denial, O Hrothgar, to gladden them with thy

---

[1]Literally "before the shoulders"—variously interpreted as implying a position before or behind the king.

converse. They seem from their war-gear worthy of the respect of earls; the leader at least, who hath led these warsmen hither, is surely goodly."

6

Hrothgar, helm of the Scyldings, spake: "I knew him as a child. His father of old was named Ecgtheow; to him Hrethel the Geat at his home gave his only daughter. Boldly now hath his son come hither, and sought out a true friend. The seafaring ones when they carried thither to the Geats costly gifts for friendly remembrance brought word that he, the bold one in war, had in his hand-grip the strength of thirty. Him, I have hope, the Holy God has sent us West Danes of His grace for aid against dread of Grendel. Gifts must I tender the good youth for his brave spirit. Make haste and bid the band of kinsmen come in together. Say to them also in fitting words they are, welcome among the Dane-folk."

Then Wulfgar went to the door of the hall, stood there and spake: "My lord, the victorious prince of the East-Danes bids me tell you he knoweth your high kinship, and that ye in his sight, ye bold in heart, are welcome hither over the sea-waves. Now may ye go in your war-gear, under your battle-masks, to see Hrothgar. Let your war-shields and spears, shafts for the killing, abide here the outcome of your converse."

Then the mighty one arose with many a man about him, a press of doughty thanes. Some remained there, as the brave one bade them, kept watch of the war-gear. Together they went speedily where the hero directed, under Heorot's roof.

The bold one went, stern beneath his helmet, till he stood within. Beowulf spake—the network of the burnie, linked by the smith's craft, gleamed upon him: "Hail to thee, Hrothgar! I am Hygelac's kinsman and war-thane. I have already in my youth essayed many deeds of prowess. To me openly were Grendel's doings made known in the land of my people. Sea-faring men say that this hall, the fairest of dwellings, stands idle and useless to all, so soon as the evening's light becometh hid 'neath the bright heaven. Then did wise men, Lord Hrothgar, the worthiest of my people, counsel that I seek thee, for they knew the strength of my might, saw it for themselves when I came from battle, blood-stained from the foe, where I bound five of them, overthrew the race of eotens, and slew the nickers by night in the waves—suffered perilous straits, repaid the hate shown the Weders (woes they endured!), put an end to their sorrows. And now I, by my single hand, shall bring Grendel, the demon, the giant one, to judgment. I desire now therefore, prince of the Bright-Danes, to ask thee one boon. Refuse me not, guardian of warriors, loved friend of the people, now I am come from so far, that I alone with my band of earls, my body of brave men, may cleanse Heorot. I have also learned that the monster in his recklessness takes no thought to use weapons: I then, so may my liege-lord, Hygelac, find pleasure in me, shall think scorn to bear sword or the broad shield, yellow-rimmed, to the battle, but with my hand-grip shall I join with the fiend and fight to the death, foe against foe. He must there, whom death taketh, believe it the Lord's award. I ween that Grendel, if he prevail, shall feast undismayed on the Geat-folk in the war-hall, as he hath oft done on the might of the Hrethmen. Thou shalt not need then to hide my head away; for Grendel will have me, stained with blood, if death take me, will bear away the bloody corse and think to devour it; he, the lone-goer, will eat it ungrieving, and smear with my blood his moor-lairs; no longer shalt thou need then to care for my body's nurture. Send to Hygelac, if warfare take me, the best of battle-weeds, goodliest of garments, that guards my breast—it was the bequest of Hrethla, and the handwork of Weland.[1] Wyrd[2] goeth ever as she must!"

7

Hrothgar, helm of the Scyldings, spake: "To be a bulwark of defence and a prop hast thou sought us, my friend Beowulf. Thy father waged the greatest of feuds; with his own hand he slew Heatholaf among the Wulfings. Then might not the kin of the Weders hold to him for fear of war. Hence sought he the folk of the South-Danes, the Honor-Scyldings, over the moil of the waves, when I first ruled the

---

[1]The famous smith of Teutonic legend.
[2]The Teutonic Fate; a personification of unalterable destiny.

Danefolk and held in my youth the treasure-city of heroes; it was when Heorogar, my elder brother, Healfdene's child, had died and was no more living—a better man was he than I. Afterward, I settled the feud for money, sending ancient treasure to the Wulfings over the back of the waters; oaths your father sware to me.

"Sorrow it is to me in soul to say to any man what despite and instant evil Grendel hath wrought me in Heorot through his malice. My hall-company, my band of warsmen, is minished; Wyrd swept them away into the horror that compasseth Grendel. God may readily stay the mad spoiler in his deeds. Full often boasted my warsmen drunken with beer, over their ale-horns, that they in the beer-hall with their dread blades would await a meeting with Grendel. Then was the mead-hall, this lordly dwelling, at morning-tide, when day grew light, stained with gore, all the bench-boards besprent with blood, the hall with the bloodshed; wherefore I had so many the fewer true thanes, warriors beloved, as death took away. Sit now to the feasting and unfold to my men thy purpose and hope of success, as thy mind may prompt thee."

Then was a bench set for the Geatmen in the hall all together. There the strong-hearted ones went to sit, in excellence of might. A thane looked to the task set him, to bear in his hands the fretted ale-stoup, and poured out the shining mead. Now and again the gleeman sang clear in Heorot. There was joy among the warriors, a worshipful company by no means small of Danes and Weders.

8

Hunferth, the son of Ecglaf, who sat at the feet of the lord of the Scyldings, spake and unloosed hidden cause of strife; great heart-burning was his because of the journey of Beowulf, the bold seafarer, for that he could not brook that any other man should ever win more of honors in the mid-earth under heaven than himself: "Art thou that Beowulf that strove against Breca, didst vie with him in swimming on the broad sea, when ye twain didst try the billows, and out of mad boastfulness risked your lives in the deep waters? Not any man, loved or loathed, might wean ye from your hazardous venture. So ye swam on the sea, covered the sea-streams with your arms, measured the sea-ways, smote with your hands, and glided over the ocean. The ocean was swollen with billows in winter's flood. In the grip of the waters ye toiled seven nights. He overmastered thee in the swimming, had the greater might. Then at morning-tide the sea bare him up among the Heatharemes, whence, dear to his people, he sought his loved home, the land of the Brondings, the fair city of peace where he had his folk, his walled town, and treasure. The son of Beanstan truly fulfilled all his boast against thee. Therefore I foresee for thee a worse outcome, a strife more grim, though thou wast ever strong in the storm of battle, if thou durst for the space of a night-time abide nigh Grendel."

Beowulf, son of Ecgtheow, spake: "Look ye, friend Hunferth, thou hast talked, drunken with beer, more than a plenty about Breca, and told of his venture. The truth I shall tell, that I had more endurance in the sea, strength in the waves, than any other man. We said when we were children, and made a vaunt of it—we were both of us still in our youth—that we would hazard our lives out upon the ocean, and it was thus we fulfilled it. We held our stout swords bare in our hands as we swam in the sea, for we thought to guard ourselves against the whale fishes. No whit might he swim ahead of me on the waves of the flood, or more swiftly in the deep; nor would I from him. We were together in the sea the space of five nights, till the flood and the rising waves, coldest of weather and night closing down in mist, drave us apart, and the north-wind, battle-fierce, came against us. Rough were the waves. The fierceness of the sea-fishes was stirred up; then was my body-sark, hard and hand-linked, a help to me against the foes; my woven battle-garment, worked with gold, lay on my breast. A fell spoiler in his wrath dragged me to the bottom, held me fast, the grim one, in his grip. Yet it was given me with my point, with my war-sword, to reach the monster. The strife did away with the mighty sea-beast by my hand.

9

"Thus the loathly raveners ceased not to press me sore. I served them as was right with my sword of price. In no wise had they joy, those workers of evil, of a full meal, to seize on me and sit round to the feast nigh the sea-bottom, for on the morrow, wounded by thrusts, slain by the sword-strokes, they lay up along the sea beach, so might they never again stay the seafarers on their way about the deep crossing.

"Light came in the east, the bright beacon of God, the waves went down, so that I might see the sea-nesses, the windy walls. Wyrd oft spareth one not marked for death, if his courage be good. Be that as it may, it was mine to slay nine nickers with the sword. Never heard I tell at night of a harder fight 'neath the vault of heaven, nor of man in worse plight in the sea-streams. Yet I got off with my life from the grip of my foes, though worn with my faring. Then the sea-flood in its streaming, the tossing billows, bare me on to the Finns' land.

"Never heard I aught of like shrewd affrays, terror of sword-play, on thy part. Never did Breca yet, or either of you, achieve in the sport of battle deed so daring with blood-stained blades (I make little boast of it), though thou wert the slayer of thine own brethren, thy chief of kin; for that thou shalt suffer thy doom in hell, whatever thy cunning. I tell thee truly, son of Ecglaf, that Grendel, the monster abhorred, would never have wrought so many horrid deeds and shameful harm in Heorot toward thy lord, were thy mind and soul so shrewdly fierce, as thou thyself dost say. But he hath found he need not dread overmuch the enmity or fierce onslaught of your people, the Victor-Scyldings. He taketh toll by force, spareth none of the Dane-folk, warreth after his lust, killeth and eateth, nor looketh for reprisal from the Spear-Danes. But the strength and prowess of the Geats shall now bid him to battle. He that may shall go afterwards proudly to the mead-drinking, when the morning-light of another day, the sun clad in brightness, shall shine forth from the south o'er the children of men."

Then the lord of the Bright-Danes, giver of treasure, gray-haired and battle-famed, was assured of succor; the shepherd of the people gave ear to Beowulf's fixed intent. There was laughter of heroes; the uproar of it sounded forth; joyous was their converse.

Wealhtheow, the queen, in her deckings of gold, went forth, mindful of courtly custom. She greeted the men in the hall, and then, as wife free-born, gave the cup first to the noble warden of the East-Danes, bade him, beloved by his people, be blithe at the beer-drinking. He, the king famed for victory, in gladness partook of the feast and the hall-cup. Then the lady of the Helmings went about to old and young in every part, gave the gemmed beaker till the time came the proud-thoughted queen, decked with her diadem, should bring the mead-cup to Beowulf. She greeted the Lord of the Geats and thanked

God with wisely-ordered words that her wish was fulfilled, in that she might put her trust in some one of earls for help in her troubles.

The warrior fierce in the fight drank of the cup at the hands of Wealhtheow, and then, made eager for the fray, gan speak in formal wise; Beowulf, son of Ecgtheow, spake: "This I purposed, when I went up on the deep, boarded the sea-craft with my fellowship, that I should either work the will of your people wholly, or fall in the fray, fast in the fiend's grip. Either will I do deeds befitting my birth or meet my last day in this mead hall." These words, the vaunt of the Geat, pleased the lady. In her deckings of gold, she passed on to sit, the free-born folk-queen, beside her lord.

Then again, as erstwhile, was brave speech spoken in the hall. In gladness were the people. The uproar rose of the victor-folk, till that the son of Healfdene had a mind suddenly to seek his evening's rest, for he knew that an onslaught was purposed on the high hall by the monster, so soon as they might no more see the sun's light, or night growing dusk over all, and creatures of the shadow-helm should come stalking, dark beneath the sky. The company all arose. Then Hrothgar greeted Beowulf, one warrior another, in set speech, wished him safe outcome, overmastery of the wine-hall, and spake this word: "Never, since I might lift hand or shield, have I ever given over in trust this mighty house of the Danes to any of men, save now to thee. Have now and hold this fairest of houses, bear thy greatness in mind, make known the might of thy prowess, watch against the foe. No lack shall be thine of things worth the having, if thou come forth with thy life from this mighty task."

10

Then Hrothgar, lord of the Scyldings, went him forth from the hall with his troop of warriors. The warrior leader would go to his rest with Wealhtheow, his wife. The Kingly Glory had set, as men have heard, a guard against Grendel in the hall. A charge apart he held in respect to the lord of the Danes, kept ward for the giant one.

Truly, the prince of the Geats put ready trust in his bold might and the Lord's grace. He took off him then his iron burnie, his helm from his head, gave his richly chased sword, choicest of blades, to his serving-thane, and bade the man keep his war-gear. Ere he mounted his bed, spake Beowulf, the worthy one of the Geats, a vaunting word: "In no wise count I myself less in battle-crafts and deeds of war than Grendel himself. Therefore I will not with the sword slay him and take his life, though the might is mine wholly. These helps—to strike at me and hew my shield—he knows not, daring though he be in deeds of malice. But we, this night, if he dare seek strife without weapons, shall lay aside the sword. And, at the end, may the wise God, the Holy Lord, award the mastery on either hand as seemeth Him meet."

Then the brave one in battle laid him down, the head-pillow received the earl's cheek, and about him many a hardy seafarer bowed him to his hall-rest.

No one of them thought that he thereafter should ever again seek his loved home, his people, or the free town where he was reared, seeing they had heard tell that, ere then, a murderous death had taken off too many by far of the Dane-folk in the wine-hall. But the Lord gave them the destiny to speed in the strife, help and aid to the people of the Weders, such that they all overcame their foe through one man's strength, the might of himself alone. The truth is made known that the Mighty God ruleth mankind from everlasting.

In the dark night came striding the walker in shadow. Those set to watch, that should guard the gabled hall, slept, all save one. It was known to men the fell spoiler might not, if the Lord willed not, swing them under the shadow. But that single one, watching in flush of wrath with swelling anger, bided the award of battle.

11

Then from the moor, from under the misty fells, came Grendel striding; God's wrath he bare. The fell spoiler planned to trap one of the race of men in the high hall. Under the clouds he went till he might see without trouble the wine-hall, the treasure-house of men, brave with gold. It was not the first time he had sought the home of Hrothgar; never, though, before or since in the days of his life found he hall-thanes more doughty. Came then making his way to the hall the warring one severed from joy. The door, fastened with bands forged in the fire, soon gave way when he laid hold of it with his hands; bent on evil, puffed up with wrath as he was, he brake open the mouth of the hall. Quickly then the fiend trod in on the shining floor, strode on, fierce of mood. An unlovely light, likest to flame, stood in his eyes. He saw in the hall many warriors sleeping, a fellowship of one blood assembled together, the throng of kinsfolk. Then his heart laughed within him. He thought, the grisly monster, ere day came, to sunder life from body of each of them, for hope of a fill of feasting had come to him. But no longer was it fate's decree that he might, after that night, feed on more of the race of men.

The kinsman of Hygelac, strong in might, watched how the fell spoiler was of mind to set about his sudden onslaughts. The monster thought not to be long about it, but for a first start seized quickly on a sleeping thane, tore him taken unawares, bit into his bone-frame, drank the blood from the veins, and swallowed him down piece by piece. Soon he had bolted all the lifeless body, hand and foot. He stepped forward nearer, took next in his hands the hero, bold of heart, on his bed. The fiend reached for him with his claw, but he grasped it with set purpose, and threw his weight on Grendel's arm. Soon found that herder of evils that never in any other man, in any corner of the earth, had he met with mightier hand grip. He was affrighted mind and heart, yet might he make off none the sooner. His one thought was to get him gone; he was minded to flee into the darkness, to seek the drove of devils. There was then for him no such doings as he before that, in earlier days, had fallen in with.

Remembered then the good kinsman of Hygelac his evening's vaunt; he stood upright and laid fast hold upon him. The fingers of the giant one snapped. He was getting free and the hero stepped forward. The mighty one meant, if so he might, to get at large, and flee away to his fen-lairs. He knew his fingers' strength was in the foeman's close grip. That was an ill journey the doer of mischief had taken to Heorot.

The lordly hall was clamorous with the din. Panic fell on all the Danes that dwelt in the city, on every bold warrior and earl. Maddened were the raging strugglers; the building re-echoed. It was great wonder, then, that the wine-hall held firm against them in their battle-rage, that it did not fall, the fair dwelling of man's making, to the earth, save that shrewd care had bound it so fast with iron bands within and without. Then, as I have heard tell, when they strove in their fury, mead-benches many, decked with gold, fell over from the raised floor. The wise ones among the Scyldings had never thought that any man of men by his might should ever shatter that fabric, passing good and made brave with bones of beasts, or spoil it through cunning, save the fire's embrace might swallow it up in smoke.

An uproar strange enough rose on high. Quaking terror lay upon the North-Danes, upon those who heard, the outcry, hearkened God's foe yelling out his stave of terror, his song of defeat, the thrall of hell bewailing his hurt. Much too tightly that one held him, who had of men the strongest might in this life's day.

12

The protector of earls would not in any wise let him that came with murder in his heart go from him alive; he counted not his life's day of price to any. Earls of his a plenty made play with their tried swords, handed down from their fathers, to save their lord's life, if in any wise they might; they knew not, those bold-hearted warsmen, when they went into the fight and thought to hew Grendel on every side and find out his soul, that not any pick of blades on earth, none of battle-bills, could touch that fell spoiler, for he had laid his spell on weapons of victory, on every keen edge. Woeful was his last end to be in this life's day, and his outlawed ghost must fare far into the fiend's grip. Then found he, that before in mirth of mood had wrought mankind many evils (he was under God's ban), that his body would avail him not, seeing that the brave kinsman of Hygelac had him by the hand; hateful to each was the other alive. The grisly monster suffered hurt of body. In his shoulder a fearful wound began to show; the sinews sprang apart, the bone-frame cracked asunder. Fame of the battle was given to Beowulf. Grendel must flee away beneath the fen-fells, sick unto death, go seek out his dwelling, reft of his comfort. He knew then the more surely that his life's end was come, his measure of days. The will of all the Danes was fulfilled by that deadly strife. He then, who had come from afar, the wise one and bold of heart, had cleansed Heorot, and saved it from peril. The prince of the Geatmen had made whole his boast to the East-Danes in that he had taken away all their trouble, the burden of spiteful hate they till then had suffered, and in stress of need must suffer, a sorrow by no means small. A manifest token of this it was, when the valorous one laid down the band, the arm and shoulder—the whole claw of Grendel was there together—beneath the broad roof.

13

In the morning, then, as I have heard tell, was there many a warrior about the mead-hall; from far and near the leaders of the people fared through the wide ways to see the marvel, the tracks of the foe. Grendel's life-ending seemed no matter for sorrow to any of those that scanned the way he trod after his undoing, how in weariness of heart, worsted in the fight, hunted forth and nigh unto death, he bare himself away then in flight to the mere of the nickers. Its flood there was seething with gore, its dread coil of waters all mingled with hot blood; the deep welled with the blood of slaughter, after that, bereft of joys, he laid down his life, his heathen soul, doomed to death, in his fen-shelter, where hell took him.

Back then from the mere on their joyful way went riding on their steeds the old tried comrades, men of valor, and many a youth likewise, the warriors on their dapple grays. There was Beowulf's glory remembered. Oft said many a one that south or north, between the seas,[1] over the wide earth, beneath the reach of the sky, no other of shield-bearers was better, or more worthy of a kingdom. No whit though truly did they cast blame on their lord and friend, the kindly Hrothgar, for he was a good king. Whiles, the bold in battle let their yellow steeds leap or race together, where the going seemed good or was known to be best; whiles, a thane of the king, a man laden with proud vaunts, who kept in mind old stories without end, found new words for them, soothly bound together—and afterward began to tell Beowulf's feat with cunning skill and in happy wise to frame well-ordered speech, add word answering to word, and told aught man might choose of what he had heard tell of Sigemund's[2] deeds of prow-

---

[1]Probably proverbial like our "East or West," "North or South"; by some considered possibly to refer specifically to the North Sea and the Baltic.

[2]The earliest recorded version of this famous exploit; here related of Sigemund, it is later, in the Icelandic *Volsunga Saga* and the German *Niebelungenlied*, attrib-

ess, many things not widely known, the strife of the son of Wæls, journeys to far lands, feuds and deeds of violence, that the children of men had not wist of readily, save Fitela were with him when he was minded to tell somewhat of such like, the uncle to his nephew—close comrades ever in every strife.

"They had slain with their swords full many of the race of the Eotens. No small glory was added to Sigemund after his death-day, seeing that, stout in battle, he slew the dragon, keeper of the treasure-hoard. Alone under the hoar stone, the son of the atheling dared the bold deed, nor was Fitela with him. None the less was it given him that his sword, lordly blade that it was, should go through the marvellous worm so it stood fast in the wall—the dragon died a bloody death. So sped the dread hero by his prowess, that he might take his joy, as he willed, of the treasure-hoard; his sea-boat he loaded, the son of Wæls, bare into the ship's bosom the bright trappings; heat made end of the dragon.[1] The shield of warriors was of free-booters most widely famed among the races of men for deeds of valor; he throve because of it in days of old.

"After Heremod's[2] battle-craft failed, his strength and his might, he was betrayed, among the Eotens, forth into the power of his foes, done away with in haste. The waves of sorrow had troubled him long; he became to his people, to all the athelings, a perilous burden. So also often, in earlier times, many a prudent man had mourned the course the bold-minded one was taking, in whom he had trusted for help against evils, whom he had looked to see thrive as the son of his lord, fall heir to his father's honors, watch over the folk, the treas-

---

uted to Sigurd, or Siegfried, his son, and thence appears, in modern literature, in Wagner's opera, the *Siegfried*, and in William Morris's *Sigurd the Volsung*. The different versions go back to a common original, and in that original the exploit may have belonged to the father, to be afterwards attracted into the greater cycle concerning his son.

[1] Referring, probably, to the dragon's own fire, which consumed him after death. The poem speaks of the dragon which Beowulf fights as scorched by his own fire; see p. 156.

[2] Heremod provides a contrast to Beowulf, as Sigemund's bravery affords a parallel. Heremod is later cited by Hrothgar in counselling Beowulf; see p. 129. Heremod, in place of cherishing his people, oppressed them, owing apparently to a dark and brooding temper, or to madness. Thus he became a perilous burden to his people, and in old age, when his strength failed, was betrayed into the hands of the Eotens, identified in general with the Jutes, and to be distinguished in the poem from the eotens, or giants.

ure, the home-city, the realm of heroes, the ancestral lands of the Scyldings. Beowulf, in that he did, was of kindlier will toward his friends and toward all; evil came on Heremod."

Now and again, striving against one another, they measured the yellow roads with their coursers. Thus was the morning light sped on and hastened by. Many a brave-minded warrior went to the high hall to see the strange wonder. The king himself, also, warden of the treasure-hoard, known for his virtues, walked in stately wise from the queen's bower with a great company, and the queen, with her train of women, paced up the path beside him to the mead-hall.

14

Hrothgar spake; he went to the hall, stood beside the pillar, looked on the steep-pitched roof, brave with gold, and Grendel's hand: "For this sight thanks be paid forthwith to the Almighty! Much of evil and harm have I suffered from Grendel. Ever may God, the Lord of Glory, work wonder on wonder. It was not long ago that I thought not forever to look for help in aught of my troubles whilst the fairest of houses stood bloodstained and gory—a woe wide-reaching for each of my wise ones who hoped not to the end of time to guard the people's fastness from foes, from ghosts, and from demons. Now hath a man through the Lord's might done a deed we might none of us compass aforetime for all our wisdom. Behold, truly, this may say even such a one of women, if she yet liveth, that hath brought forth this son among the races of men, that the everlasting God hath been gracious to her in her child-bearing. Now will I love thee, Beowulf, best of men, as a son in my heart; hold thou close henceforth this new kinship. No lack shall be thine of things worth having in the world, that I have at my bidding. Full oft for less service have I given award of treasured riches to a warrior not so worthy, one weaker in battle. Thou hast wrought for thyself by thy deeds that thy fame shall live for ever and ever. May the Almighty requite thee with good, as till now He hath done!"

Beowulf spake, the son of Ecgtheow: "Full gladly in thy service have we carried through this mighty task, this fight; boldly we dared the strength of the unknown. I wish mightily thou couldst have seen him, the foe himself in his trappings, bowed to his fall. I thought

to bind him full speedily with hard bonds on his death-bed, so that
he through the grip of my hands should lie toiling for his life, save
his body should slip away. I could not, since the Lord willed it not,
cut him off from his going; I held him not fast enough, the deadly
foe—much too strong was the fiend in his footing. Yet for his life's
fending he left behind him his claw to mark his path, his arm, and
his shoulder; none the less might he buy there, in his need, no com-
fort, nor shall he, because of it, live the longer, the loathly spoiler,
burdened with sins, for his hurt hath straitly clutched him in its close
grip with bonds of bale. There the outcast, in the guilt of his sins,
shall abide the great judgment, as the Lord in His splendor is minded
to mete it unto him."

Then in his vaunting speech was the warrior, the son of Ecglaf,
more quiet concerning deeds of war, after that the athelings had
seen, each of them there before him above the high roof, through the
earl's might, the hand and fingers of the fiend. Most like to steel was
each strong nail, the hand-spurs of the heathen one, the monstrous
barbs of the foeman. Each one said that no blade of doughty men,
though ever so good, would have so laid hold of him as to shear away
the battle-fist, all bloody, of the monster.

15

Then forthwith was Heorot bidden to be decked inwardly by the hand;
many of them there were, of men and of women, that made ready the
wine-hall, the guest-house. Gleaming with gold shone the hangings
on the wall, wondrous things many to see for any one that looketh at
such things. The bright house was much broken, all fastened though
it was within with iron bands. The hinges were wrenched away; the
roof alone was left all whole, when the monster, guilty of deeds of
outrage, hopeless of life, had turned to flee. Not easy is it to flee away,
let him do it that will, for each that hath a soul of the children of men
dwelling on earth must needs strive toward the place made ready for
him, forced on him by fate, where his body shall sleep, fast in its bed
of rest, after life's feasting.

Then was it the time and hour that the son of Healfdene should
go to the hall; the king himself desired to eat of the feast. Never

heard I of a people with a greater host bear themselves more becomingly about their treasure-giver. In the pride of their renown they bowed them to the benches, rejoiced in the plenty. In fair wise their kinsmen, the valorous-hearted Hrothgar and Hrothulf, drank in the high hall many a mead-cup. Heorot was filled within with friends; in no wise at this time had the Folk-Scyldings wrought wickedness.

Then, in reward for his victory, the son of Healfdene gave to Beowulf a golden standard, a broidered war-banner, a helmet and burnie; a mighty treasure-sword full many saw borne before the warrior. He needed not feel shame before the bowsmen for the gifts given him for his keeping; never heard I of many men that gave to others on the mead-bench four treasures in friendlier wise. About the helmet's crown, a raised ridge without, wound with small rods, maintained a guard for the head, that the file-furnished blades, hard of temper, might not harm it in their boldness, when the warrior with shield must go forth against his foes. Then the safeguard of earls bade eight steeds, their bridles heavy with gold, be led indoors on the floor of the hall; on one of them rested a saddle, fashioned with cunning art and well-dight with treasure, that had been the battle-seat of the high king when the son of Healfdene had will to wage the swordplay; never at the front failed the far-famed one's battle-might, when the slain were falling. And then the prince of the Ingwines gave Beowulf the right over both of these, the steeds and the weapons, bade him have good joy of them. In such wise, manfully, the mighty prince, treasure-warden of heroes, paid for shocks of battle with steeds and treasure, such as none might ever belie that hath will to speak the truth according to the right.

16

Further, then, the lord of earls gave treasure on the mead-bench, swords handed down from old, to each of the earls that had drawn over the sea-way with Beowulf, and bade that payment be made with gold for the one that Grendel first wickedly slew, as he would have slain more of them had not the wise God and the hero's daring forestalled that fate for them. The Lord ruled all the children of men, as He now still doth; therefore is wise understanding and forethought of mind best everywhere. He who for long in these days of strife maketh use of the world must undergo much of good and evil.

Song and sound of playing were joined together there before the battle-leader of the Half-Danes. The play-wood was touched, the lay oft rehearsed, what time Hrothgar's gleeman must duly call forth the hall-joy along the mead-bench:

"Through the sons of Finn,[1] when the onslaught came on them,

---

[1] A brief summary of a story known to have existed in an epic of some length among the Anglo-Saxons from a fragment found in Lambeth Palace. This fine fragment runs as follows:

"... the gables surely are not burning?" Spake then the king, young in battle: "Day dawneth not from the east, nor here doth a dragon fly, nor here are the gables of this hall aflame, but they bear forth the boar, the birds of battle sing, the gray burnie ringeth, the war-wood maketh clamor, shield answereth shaft. Now shineth the moon, wandering behind the clouds; now deeds of woe take their beginning that shall give rise to the vengeful hatred of this people. But waken ye now, my warriors, have your shields in hand, be forward in the fight, be brave."

Then rose many a thane, well dight with gold, girded on them their swords. The lordly warriors Sigeferth and Eaha went then to the doors, and drew their swords, and Ordlaf and Guthlaf went to be at the other doors, and Hengest himself followed in their lead.

Then Garnef urged Guthere that they should not in the first onset bear in harness life so noble to the doors of the hall, now the warrior stout in battle was minded to despoil it, but he asked, the warrior bold of heart, before them all in no secret wise who held the door: "Sigeferth is my name," said he; "I am prince of the Secges, a freebooter known far and wide. Many a sorrow have I lived through and sore encounter; still is assured thee here whatsoever thou thyself wilt seek from me."

Then at the wall was there din of mortal conflict; the curved shield in the hands of the valiant must needs shatter the bone-helm. The hall-floor resounded, till in the fight Garnef, son of Guthlaf, fell first of earth-dwellers there, and about him many good men. The raven wheeled on the wing about the slain, wandered swart and dusky-gleaming. The flash of the swords was as if all Finnesburh were afire. Never heard I tell of sixty victor-warriors bearing themselves in strife of warsmen more worthily and better, nor ever did swains pay better for the sweet mead than did his warrior-folk pay Hnæf.

Five days they fought in such wise that none of their fellowship fell; but they held the doors. There went then a wounded warrior away, said his burnie was broken, his battle-mail made of none avail, and his helmet thrust through as well. Then straightway asked him the shepherd of the people how the warriors had come forth from their wounds, or which of the youths....

A reconstruction of the story from the version in *Beowulf* and this fragment is beset with difficulties, the proper translation of both being in several places a

must Hnaef the Scylding, famed warrior of the Half-Danes, in the Frisian slaughter meet with his fall. Hildeburh had truly no need to praise the good faith of the Eotens; not by her fault was she bereaved of her dear sons and brothers in the shield-play; one after another they fell, wounded by the spear; a sorrowful woman was she!

"It was not for naught, surely, the daughter of Hoc bemoaned the decree of fate after morning came, when she might see beneath the sky the murderous overthrow of her kinsmen, where till then earth's greatest joy was hers.

War took off all Finn's thanes, save only a few, so that he might no whit wage war on the battle-field with Hengest, nor save by warfare the poor leavings of his band from the thane of the prince. But they offered the Danes a pact, that they would fit for themselves in every wise another hearth floor, a hall, and a high seat, so might the Danes have equal power with themselves, the children of the Eotens, and each day, at the giving of gifts, the son of Folcwalda would treat the Danes worshipfully, show regard for Hengest's fellowship, by giving of rings, and even so much of precious treasure of plates of gold, as that wherewith he would cheer the Frisian kindred in the beer-hall.

"Then they plighted on either side a fast troth of peace. Finn

---

matter of doubt and the account in *Beowulf* merely a rapid outline. Two typical attempts that have won some acceptance are as follows.

Finn, the Frisian, having carried off Hoc's daughter, Hildeburh, is pursued by Hoc, who is killed. Hnæf and Hengest, his sons, when grown of age, invade Finn's country seeking revenge, and in the battle which ensues so many are killed on both sides that a compact of peace is made. Hnæf has been killed, but Hengest, remaining with his men till the spring, broods on revenge and does not go when spring comes. The Frisians, perceiving his half-formed design, fall upon him at night in the hall and, in the attack described in part in the fragment above, slay all his men except Guthlac and Oslaf, who escape and return with an army, slay Finn, and carry Hildeburh back to her own land.

The second version is that Finn has married Hildeburh, and Hnæf, her brother, is staying with her. A quarrel takes place, and Hnæf falls in a night attack (that of the fragment). A compact of peace is made, one condition being that the feud is not to be spoken of. Hengest, however, secretly designs revenge, and with this intent treacherously becomes Finn's liegeman (see footnote [1], p. 118). Later, Guthlac and Oslaf, sent for aid by Hengest, return with a fresh body of Danes, Finn is killed, and Hildeburh carried away.

The latter version, in various forms, is now more generally accepted, but so many difficult points are involved that it is best to consider the whole matter still unsettled.

vowed to Hengest by oaths, solemnly and in true earnest, he would hold in honor the poor few that were left of Hengest's followers under the ruling of his wise men; that no man there should break the pact by word or deed, or ever through crafty intent call it to mind, though they, bereft of their prince, should, since it was thus forced on them, follow him that slew their ring-giver; if, moreover, any of the Frisians with reckless speech should call that mortal hate to mind, then the sword's edge should avenge it.

"The oath was made, and the treasured gold fetched from the hoard. The best warsman of the Battle-Scyldings was ready at the fire; on the pile was plain to see the blood-stained sark, the swine all of gold, the boar-helmet of tough iron, and many an atheling, dead of his wounds, that fell in the slaughter.

"Then Hildeburh bade her own son be given to the flames on Hnaef's pyre, his body to the burning, and be put on the fire. The poor woman wept on his shoulder, sorrowed for him in song. The warrior went up on the pile. The greatest of death-fires whirled up to the clouds, roared before the barrow; the heads melted, the slashes broke apart, when the blood sprang, out from the body's deadly wounds. The flame, greediest of spirits, swallowed up all those whom death had taken off of both peoples; from them both had their strength been taken away."

17

"Then the warfarers, despoiled of their friends, went to seek out living-places, to see Friesland, its homesteads and its high city. Hengest then still, through that death-stained winter, dwelt with Finn in every wise without strife. He kept thought of his home, though he might not drive his ringed prow over the sea. The deep was swollen with storm, dark with the wind. Winter locked the waves in its icy shackles, till another year came to the homes of men, as it now still doth, the seasons, glory-bright that ever hold to the times set them.

"Then was winter away, and fair the earth's bosom. The guest in his exile was meaning to go from that land; but he thought rather of vengeance than of the sea-voyage, if so be he might bring about a meeting in anger, that he might take his account therein of the sons of the Eotens. Thus it was[1] he escaped not the law of this world when Hun plunged Lafing into his breast, his battle-gleamer, best of swords, whose edges were well-known to the Eotens.

"Likewise thereafter a fierce death by the sword found out Finn, the bold of heart, in his own home, after that Guthlaf and Oslaf, come home over the sea, had told in sorrow of the grim strife, and blamed on him the many sorrows that had befallen them. He might not keep his wavering spirit in his breast. The hall was covered then with the bodies of the foe, and Finn likewise was slain, the king among his fellowship, and his queen taken. The bowsmen of the Scyldings bare to the ships all the household goods of the country's king, all they might find in Finn's house of precious ornaments and cunningly set gems. Over the sea-way—they bare the princely lady to the Danes, led her to her people."

The lay was sung, the gleeman's song. Again rose the revel, the clamor along the benches resounded clear, the bearers gave of the wine from vessels of wondrous workmanship. Then came forth Wealhtheow under her golden diadem, going where the goodly twain, uncle and nephew, were seated; as yet they were at peace[2] together, each loyal to the other. There likewise sat Hunferth, the spokesman, at the feet of the lord of the Scyldings; all of them had faith in his mettle, that he had a high spirit, though he had not been steadfast to his kinsfolk in the sword-play.

Then spake the lady of the Scyldings: "Take this cup, my liege-lord, giver of treasure. Be thou of glad heart, generous friend of men, and speak to the Geats with words of kindness. So should one do. Be gracious towards the Geats, mindful of gifts, now that thou hast peace near and far. They have told me that thou desirest to hold this warrior as thy son. Heorot, the bright hall of ring-giving, is cleansed; take thy joy of giving, whilst thou mayest, many rewards, and leave

---

[1]This passage has been variously interpreted in conjunction with the several attempts which have been made to recover the story. In connection with the first of the versions above it is construed to mean that Hengest was slain by Finn with a sword, Hunlafing, or by Hun (a follower of Finn; the name occurs in "Widsith") with a sword, Lafing. In connection with the second version, it is interpreted to mean that Hengest through craft did not refuse to become Finn's liegeman, when (as a ceremonial act) Finn laid Hunlafing (his sword) on his breast, or when Hun (as above), acting for Finn, laid Lafing (a sword) on his breast.

[2]The story implied here is not known. The nephew is Hrothulf.

folk and realm to thy kinsmen, when thou must forth to meet thy
fate. I know my gracious Hrothulf, that he will keep in honorable
charge the youth, if thou, friend of the Scyldings, shouldst leave the
world before him. I ween he will repay our children with good, if he
keep thought of all we have done in the past at his wish and for his
behoof, since he was still but a child."

Then she turned to the bench where her sons were, Hrethric
and Hrothmund, and the sons of warriors, the youth there together.
There by the two brothers sat the goodly one, Beowulf, the Geat.

18

A cup was borne to him, and pledges proffered with friendly speech,
and twisted gold laid before him in token of gracious regard, with
two arm-jewels, a coat of mail, rings, and the fairest of collars I have
heard tell of on earth—of none fairer heard I under the sky among the
hoarded treasures of heroes, after that Hama bare off to the bright
city the collar of the Brosings,[1] the jewel and coffer, fled the evil wiles
of Eormanric, and chose eternal gain. Hygelac the Geat, grandson of
Swerting, had this collar on his last foray,[2] when beneath his standard
he guarded his treasure, kept ward of his battle-spoil; him Wyrd took
away, after that he, for his foolhardiness, had undergone woes and
vengeance at the hands of the Frisians. The lord of the realm carried
with him at that time this adornment and its precious stones, over the
cup of the waves. He fell beneath his shield, and the king's body came
into the Franks' grasp, and his breast-mail and the collar as well. The
fighting-men of less degree despoiled the corse after the battle's end.
The people of the Geats filled the abode of the dead.

The hall caught up the clamor of the revel. Wealhtheow made
discourse, and spake before the company: "Take thy joy in this col-
lar, dear Beowulf, youth blessed of fortune, and use this mail and
these treasures of the people, and thrive well. Give proof of thyself

---

[1]The *Brisingamen* of the Eddas, or jewelled collar of the goddess Freyja. Hama is
known in Germanic legend as Heime, but not this story. Eormenric is the great
Hermanric of history, king of the Ostrogoths.
[2]Hygelac's foray against the Frisians.

by thy might and be friendly in giving counsel to these youths; I shall keep in mind thy due therefor. Thou hast so wrought that far and near, forever henceforth, men shall pay thee honor, even so far as the sea enfoldeth its windy walls. Be, whilst thou livest, an atheling blest with wealth; I heartily wish thee holdings of treasure. Be thou helpful in doing for my son, guarding his welfare. Here is each earl true to the other, wild of mood, loyal to his liege-lord. The thanes are willing, the people in every wise ready at bidding. Ye warriors well-drunken, do ye as I bid."

Then went she to her place. There was the choicest of feasts. The men drank of the wine; of Wyrd they reeked not, the grim doom fixed from aforetime, as it had come to many an earl. When that even came and Hrothgar went him, the ruler, to his rest, in his house, unnumbered earls kept ward of the hall, as they oft had done before. They bared the bench-floor and it was spread through its length with beds and pillows. Ready and doomed for death, one of the beer-servers bowed him to his rest in the hall. They set at their heads their battle-targes, the framed wood of their bright shields. There, over each atheling, were plain to see on the bench the helmet lifted in battle, the ringed burnie, the mighty shafts in their strength. It was their rule to be ever and again ready for the fray at home or in wartime, either one, even at what time soever need might befall their liege-lord. That was a good people!

19

They sank then to sleep. One paid sorely for his evening's rest, even as full often had befallen them after Grendel took the gold-hall for his own, did what was not right till the end came, death following upon his sins. It became plain, and known far and wide of men, that an avenger still lived even yet after him, the loathly one, for a long time following upon that bitter warfare. Grendel's mother kept thought of her sorrow, a she-one, a monster-wife, that was fated to dwell midst the water's terrors, in the cold streams, after Cain had slain by the sword his only brother, his kin by one father—outlawed he went away then, with the mark of murder on him, to flee the joys of men, and dwelt in waste places. Of him were born many demons ordained of fate; Grendel was one of them, an outcast filled with hatred, who found at

Heorot a man watching, awaiting battle. There the monster came to grips with him, but he was mindful of the strength of his might, the deep-seated gift God had given him, and trusted him for grace in the Almighty, for comfort and aid; hence he overcame the fiend, felled the demon of hell. Then went he forth, that foe of mankind, abject and reft of joy, to look on the house of death. And, still thereafter, his mother, greedy, and dark of mood, was of mind to go a journey fraught with grief to avenge the death of her son, came therefore to Heorot, where the Ring-Danes slept in the hall.

Then when Grendel's mother made her way in, was there straight-way there for the earls a turning backward to what had been before. The terror was less even by so much as is woman's strength, the fierce-ness of a woman in fight, beside a weapon-bearer's, when the sword bound with gold, wrought with the hammer, the blade blood stained, sheareth with its tough edge the swine that standeth above the helmet.

Then in the hall from above the benches was the hard-edged sword taken down, many a broad shield lifted in the hand's grip; they whom the terror seized took no thought of helmet or broad burnie. The monster was in haste, would thence away to save her life, for that she was discovered. Quickly had she one of the athelings fast in her clutch, and went off to the fen. He whom she slew at his rest was a strong shield-warrior, a warsman of enduring fame, of all the men in office of comrade the dearest to Hrothgar between the seas. Beowulf was not there, for before then, after the treasure-giving, another resting-place had been fixed upon for the mighty Geat. There was outcry in Heorot. She had taken in its gore the hand of Grendel that so much had been made of. Sorrow was begun anew, was come again to their homes. The bargain was not good, seeing they must on either hand make purchase with the lives of friends.

Then was the old king, the hoar warrior, stricken in spirit when he knew his chief thane, the one dearest to him, to be lifeless and dead. Beowulf, the warrior crowned with victory, was quickly fetched to the bower. At daybreak, he, together with his earls, the highborn warrior himself with his followers, went where the wise king awaited if so be, after tidings thus grievous, the Almighty might ever will to work a change for him. The hero tried in battle went then with his fellowship over the floor—the timbered hall rang—to give words of greeting to the wise lord of the Ingwines, asked him, as courtesy bade, if his night had been peaceful.

20

Hrothgar, helm of the Scyldings, spake: "Ask not concerning that which gives joy. Sorrow is renewed among the Dane-folk. Dead is Æschere, Yrmenlaf's elder brother, my counsellor and adviser, the comrade who stood shoulder to shoulder with me when we kept guard of our heads in battle, when the footmen met together, and boar-helms clashed. Such an atheling, passing good, as Æschere was, should an earl be. The murderous demon, the wandering one, with her hand hath slain him in Heorot. I know not what path from here the fell one hath taken, glorying in her carrion food, glad of her fill. She hath avenged thine onslaught, that thou didst kill Grendel yesternight in pitiless wise by thy close grip, for that he long had minished and slain my people. Guilty of death, he fell in battle, and now hath a second come, a spoiler mighty for mischief; she is minded to avenge her kins-man, and hath carried her vengeance so far that it may seem torment of spirit hard to bear to many a thane that sorroweth in his soul for his treasure-giver. Now the hand lieth helpless that was earnest to thee of aught whatsoever that is worth the having.

"I have heard the dwellers in the land, my people, they that hold sway in their halls, say they have seen such twain as these, mighty prowlers along the borders of the homes of men, making the moors their own. One of these was, so far as they might most carefully judge, in form like a woman: the other misbegotten one trod in man's shape the path of exile, save that he was greater in size than any man. Him in days of old the earth-dwellers named Grendel: they knew not his father, or whether any lurking demons were ever born to him. They take as theirs a country hidden away, the wolf-fells and windy nesses, perilous fen-ways, where the flood of the mountain-stream goeth downward under the earth beneath the mists of the forelands. It is not far hence, measured in miles, where the mere standeth. Rime-covered thickets hang over it; a wood fast-rooted shadoweth the waters. There may a fearful marvel be seen each night, a fire in the flood. None liveth ever so wise of the children of men that knoweth the bottom. Though the rover of the heath, the stag, strong with his antlers, may seek, hunted from afar, that thick wood, he will yield up his spirit first, his life on its brink, ere he will hide away his head within it. The place is not goodly.

"Thence riseth a coil of waters dark to the clouds, when the wind stirreth up foul weather till the air groweth thick and the heavens make outcry.

"Now, again, is help in thee alone. That country thou know'st not yet, the fearsome place, where thou mayest find the much-sinning one. Seek it if thou darest. I shall requite thee for the strife with gifts for the keeping, with old-time treasures and twisted gold, as I did before, shouldst thou come thence away."

21

Beowulf spake, the son of Ecgtheow: "Sorrow not, man of wise mind! It is better one should avenge his friend than mourn for him long. Each of us must abide life's end in this world. Let him that may, win fame ere death; that shall be best thereafter for a warrior, when life is no more.

"Arise, warden of the realm, let us go quickly to look upon the track of Grendel's fellow. I promise thee he shall not flee to shelter, not in earth's bosom, or mountain forest, or ocean's bed, go where he will. For this day have patience in thine every woe, as I ween thou wilt."

Then the old man sprang up and gave thanks to God, the mighty Lord, for that the hero had spoken. A horse then, a steed with plaited mane, was bridled for Hrothgar. The wise king went in state; with him fared forth a foot-band of shield-bearers. The tracks were plain to see far along the forest-ways, the path she hath taken across the levels; straight went she over the murky moor, bare away, with his soul gone from him, the best of Hrothgar's kindred that with him governed the homestead.

Then over the steep stone-fells and narrow tracks, in close by-paths, an unknown way, by beetling cliffs and many a nicker's lair, went the son of athelings. With a few wise-minded men, he went before to see the place, till he found suddenly the mountain trees, the joyless wood, leaning over the hoar rock. The water stood beneath, blood-stained and troubled. It was for all the Danes, for the friends of the

Scyldings, a sorrow of soul to bear, grief to many a thane and every earl, when they came upon the head of Æschere on the sea-cliff. The flood boiled, as the people gazed upon it, with blood and hot gore.

The horn at times sang its stirring lay of battle. All the band sat them down. They saw in the water many of the dragon kind, strange sea-drakes making trial of the surge, likewise on the jutting rocks the nickers lying, that oft at hour of dawn make foray grief-giving on the sail-road, and dragons and wild beasts beside. In bitter wrath and swollen with fury, these hasted away; they heard the call, the war-horn singing. The prince of the Geats severed the life from one with a bow, as it strove with the sea, so that the stout battle-shaft went home to its life. Slower was it then in swimming the deep, seeing death had gripped it. Then quickly was it hemmed in closely in the waves with boar-spears keen-barbed, assailed with shrewd thrusts, and drawn on the headland, the wondrous wave-lifter. The men gazed on the fearsome unfriendly thing.

Then Beowulf put on him his earl's armor: in no wise had he misgivings for his life. His war-burnie hand-woven, broad and cunningly adorned, that could well shield his body so battle-grip might not harm his breast or the foe's shrewd clasp his life, must needs make trial of the deeps. But his head the white helmet guarded, that must mingle with the sea-depths, seek the coil of the surges, well-dight as it was with treasure-work, bound with lordly chains, as the weapon-smith wrought it in far-off days, decked it with wonders, set it with swine-shapes, that thereafter brand nor battle blade might bite it. Not least of these great helps was that which Hrothgar's spokesman had loaned him in his need; the hafted sword was named Hrunting. It was one of the chiefest of old-time treasures. Its edge was iron, dyed with poison-twigs, hardened with blood; never in battle did it betray any that clasped it in hand, durst tread the ways of terror, the meeting-place of the foe. That was not the first time it should do a deed of prowess. Surely the son of Ecglaf in the might of his strength kept not thought of what he before spake, drunken with wine, when he lent that weapon to a warrior better with the sword than he. He durst not himself hazard his life beneath the waves, striving to do a warrior's duty: thereby he forfeited the honor, the acclaims of prowess. Not so was it with the other, after he had arrayed himself for the strife.

22

Beowulf spake, the son of Ecgtheow: "Keep thou now in mind, great son of Healfdene, wise prince, freehanded friend of men, now I am ready for my venture, that of which we already have spoken, that, should I for thy need be shorn of life, thou wouldst ever be to me, gone hence away, in the place of a father. Be thou a guardian to my thanes, my close comrades, if the strife take me. Likewise send the treasures thou gavest me, dear Hrothgar, to Hygelac; then may the lord of the Geats, the son of Hrethel, know by the gold and see, when he looketh on the treasure, that I found a giver of rings goodly in manly virtues, had joy of him whilst I might. And do thou let Hunferth, warrior famed afar, have his precious war-sword with its tough edge, handed down from old. I shall win fame for myself with Hrunting, or death shall take me."

After these words the prince of the Weder-Geats hasted in his valor, would in no wise await an answer; the coil of the waters laid hold of the warrior. It was a day's while ere he might see the bottom-level. Soon she, that, ravenous for food, grim and greedy, had held for half a hundred winters the stretches of the flood, found that some one of men was there from above searching out the home of beings not man-like. She laid hold then upon him, seized him in her terrible claws. His hale body she hurt not thereby: his mail without shielded him round, so she might not, with her loathly fingers, reach through his war-coat, the linked battle-sark. The sea-wolf, when she came to the bottom, bare him then, the ring-giving prince, to her home, in such wise he might not, brave as he was, wield his weapons, though, because of it, many strange beings pressed him close in the deep, many a sea-beast with its fighting-tushes brake his battle-sark, harried their troubler.

Then the earl was aware he was in one knows not what fearsome hall, where no water might harm him aught, or the quick grip of the flood touch him because of the roofed hall. He saw the light of fire, a flashing flare brightly shining. The worthy one looked then on the she-wolf of the sea-bottom, the mighty water-wife. The full strength of onset he gave with his battle-axe, his hand held not back from the stroke, so that on her head the ring-decked blade sang out its greedy war-song. The foe found then that the battle-gleamer would not bite, or harm her life, for its edge betrayed the prince in his need. Erstwhile had it gone through many a close encounter, cloven oft the helm and battle-mail of the doomed; for the first time then did the dear treasure lay down its glory. Still was the kinsman of Hygelac, mindful of proud deeds, of one thought, and in no wise lost courage. In wrath the warrior threw aside the chased sword, strong and steel-edged, set with jewels, that it lay on the earth; he trusted to his strength, to the might of his handgrip. So must a man do when he thinketh to reach in battle enduring fame; he careth naught for his life.

Then the lord of the War-Geats—he shrank not at all from the strife—seized Grendel's mother by the shoulders. Strong in battle he hurled his life's foe, for that he was swollen with wrath, so she fell to the ground. Quickly she paid him back his dues to his hand in savage clinchings, and laid hold upon him. Spent in spirit, the fighter on foot, strongest of warriors, tripped so he fell. Then she threw herself on the stranger in her hall, and drew her dagger broad and bright-edged—she thought to avenge her son, her only child. His woven breast-mail lay on his shoulder; it shielded his life, withstood the in-thrust of point and blade. Then had the son of Ecgtheow, foremost fighter of the Geats, gone to his death beneath the broad deeps, had not his battle-burnie, the stout battle-mesh, given him help, and Holy God, the Wise Lord, Ruler of the Heavens, held sway over victory in battle, awarded it aright. Readily thereafter he found his feet.

23

He saw then among the war-gear a blade oft victorious, an old sword of the eotens, doughty of edge, one prized by warriors; it was the choicest of weapons, save that it was greater than any other man might bear out to the battle-play, good and brave to see, the work of giants. The warrior of the Scyldings seized it by its chain-bound hilt. Raging and battle-fierce, he drew the ring-marked blade, and despairing of life smote so wrathfully that the hard edge gripped her by the neck, brake the bone-rings; the sword went clean through her fated body, and she fell to the ground.

The sword was bloody; the hero gloried in his deed. The fire flamed forth; light stood within there, even as when the candle of the sky shineth brightly from heaven. He looked about the dwelling, turned him then to the wall. The thane of Hygelac, wrathful and steadfast of thought, raised the hard weapon by the hilt. The edge was not useless to the warrior, for he was minded to requite Grendel speedily for the many onslaughts he had made on the West-Danes far oftener than a single time, when he slew Hygelac's hearth-comrades in their sleep, ate fifteen men as they slept of the Dane-folk, and bare off as many more, a loathly spoil. Beowulf, relentless warrior, so far paid Grendel his dues for that, that he now saw him lying on his bed, battle-weary and lifeless, in such wise as the strife in Heorot had scathed him. The corse sprang far when it underwent a blow after death, a hard sword stroke, and Beowulf cut off the head.

Soon the men of wise thought, who with Hrothgar looked on the water, saw that the swirl of the wave was all mingled with blood, that the flood was stained with it. The white-haired old men spake together of the goodly atheling, how they looked not he should come again, glorying in victory, to seek their mighty prince, for, because of the blood, it seemed to many that the sea-wolf had slain him. Then came the ninth hour of the day. The brave Scyldings left the cliff; the gold-giving friend of men went him homeward. The strangers sat there, sick at heart, and stared on the mere. They wished and yet trusted not, to see their dear lord's self.

Then the war-brand, the sword, began, because of the monster's blood, to fall away in battle-icicles; a marvel was it how it all melted likest to ice, when the Father, that holdeth sway over times and seasons, freeth the bonds of the frost, unwindeth the flood's fetters. He is the true Lord.

The chief of the Weder-Geats took no more of the treasure-holdings in the dwelling, though he saw many there, but only the head, and with it, the sword's hilt, brave with gold; the sword had already melted, its chased blade burned wholly, so hot was the blood, so poisonous the demon of strange kind, that met her death there in the hall.

Soon was he swimming, that had borne erstwhile the battle-shock of the foe. He dove up through the water. The moil of the waves was all cleansed, the wide domains where the strange demon had yielded up her life's day and this world that passeth.

The safeguard of seafarers, the strong of heart, came swimming then to land; he joyed in his sea-spoil, the mighty burden he had with him. Then went they to him, his chosen band of thanes; God they thanked, had joy of their lord, for that it was given them to see him safe. Speedily then the helmet and burnie of the unfaltering one were loosed. The pool, the water beneath the clouds, stained with the blood of slaughter, grew still.

Forth thence they fared by the foot-paths, joyful of heart. The men measured the earth-way, the well-known road, bold as kings. The head they bare from the sea-cliff with toil that was heavy for any of them, great of courage though they were; four it took to bear Grendel's head with labor on the shaft of death to the gold-hall, till to the hall came faring forthwith the fourteen Geats, picked men brave in battle. Their liege-lord together with them trod boldly in the midst of them the meadow-stretches.

Then the foremost of the thanes, the man brave of deed, exalted in glory, the warrior bold in strife, came in to greet Hrothgar. Grendel's head, grisly to behold, was borne into the hall, where the men were drinking before the earls and the lady as well. The men looked on that sight strange to see.

24, 25[1]

Beowulf spake, the son of Ecgtheow: "Lo, with joy we have brought thee, son of Healfdene, lord of the Scyldings, in token of glory, the sea-spoil thou here beholdest. Not easily came I forth with my life, hazarded with sore hardship the toils of war beneath the waters. Almost had the strife been ended, save that God shielded me. Naught might I achieve with Hrunting in the strife, good as that weapon is, but the Ruler of Men vouchsafed it me to see hanging on the wall an old sword, noble and mighty—most oft is He guide to the friendless—so that I drew the weapon. Then I slew in the struggle the guardians of the hall, for the chance was given me. The battle-blade then, the

---

[1]The 25th division of the poem, marked in the manuscript at line 1740, begins apparently in the middle of a sentence ("till that within him a deal of overweening pride," etc.; see p. 130), and the two divisions are here, accordingly, run together.

chased sword, was burned to naught, when the blood sprang forth, hottest of battle-gore; I bare away thence the hilt from my foes, avenged in fitting wise their evil deeds and the Danes' death-fall. I promise thee, therefore, thou mayest in Heorot sleep free from care with thy fellowship of warriors, and every thane of thy people likewise, young and old—that thou needest not, lord of the Scyldings, have dread of death-peril for them on this hand, for thine earls, as thou didst ere this." Then the golden hilt, the work of giants long ago, was given into the hand of the old prince, the white-haired battle-leader. After the overthrow of the devilish ones, it fell, the work of marvellous smiths, into the keeping of the Danes' lord; when the grim-hearted one, God's foe, with murder upon him, gave up the world, and his mother also, it fell in this wise into the keeping of the best of world-kings, between the seas, of those that in Scedenig parted gifts of gold.

Hrothgar spake, looked on the hilt, the old heirloom, on which was written the beginning of that far-off strife, when the flood, the streaming ocean, slew the giant kind—they had borne themselves lawlessly. The people were estranged from the Eternal Lord; the Wielder, therefore, gave them their requital through the whelming of the waters. So was it duly lined in rimed staves on the guard of gleaming gold, set down and told for them for whom that sword was wrought, choicest of blades, with twisted hilt and decked with dragon-shapes.

Then the wise one spake, the son of Healfdene; all were silent: "That, lo, may he say that worketh truth and right among the people (the old warden of the realm keepeth all in mind from of old) that this earl was born of a nobler race. Thy fame is exalted, my friend Beowulf, among every people throughout the wide ways. Wholly with quietness dost thou maintain it, thy might with wisdom of heart. I shall fulfil my troth to thee, that we spake of, ere now, together. Thou shalt be in every wise a comfort, long-established, to thy people, a help to the warriors. Heremod was not so to the children of Ecgwela, the Honor-Scyldings. He grew not up to do as they would have him, but to cause death-fall and deadly undoing for the Dane-folk. In the swelling anger of his heart he slew his table-companions, they that stood at his shoulder, till he went alone, the mighty prince, from the joys of men. Though the mighty God raised him up and set him forth in the joys of dominion and gifts of strength above other men, none the less there grew in his mind and soul a blood-greed. He gave out rings to the Danes not at all as befitted his high estate, lived joyless, and so suffered stress for his vengeful doings, a fate long-enduring at the hands of his people. Do thou learn by this. Lay hold upon manly worth. As one wise in years, I have framed thee this discourse.

"A marvel it is how mighty God in the greatness of His soul bestoweth wise judgment on mankind, land-holdings and earlship; He hath rule over all. Whiles letteth He the heart's thought of a man of high race turn to having and holding, giveth him the joys of this world in his country, a fastness-city of men to keep, so contriveth for him that he ruleth parts of the earth, a wide realm, such that he may not know the bounds thereof. He dwelleth in fatness; sickness nor age turn him aside no whit; preying sorrow darkeneth not his soul, nor doth strife show itself anywhere, nor warring hate, but all the world wendeth to his will. He knoweth not the worse, till that within him a deal of overweening pride groweth and waxeth, while the warder sleepeth, shepherd of the soul. Too fast is that sleep, bound round with troubles; very nigh is the slayer that in grievous wise shooteth with his bow. Then is he smitten in the breast, with his helmet upon him, by a bitter shaft.

"He cannot guard him from the devious strange biddings of the Accursed Fiend. That seemeth him too little which he hath long held. Perverse of mind, he is greedy, giveth not at all out of pride the rings of plate-gold, and he forgetteth and taketh no heed of the fate to come, because of the deal of blessings God, the King of Glory, hath already given him. Therefore, at the end, it happeneth that the fleeting body sinketh and falleth, marked for death. Another taketh over the earl's former holdings, who dealeth out treasure without repining, and shall take no thought for fear.

"Guard thee from death-dealing malice, dear Beowulf, best of men, and choose the better, the eternal gain. Give not thyself to over-pride, O warrior renowned. Now is the flower of thy strength for one while; soon shall it be hereafter that sickness or the sword's edge, foe's clutch or flood's whelm, the sword's grip or the spear's flight, or grievous old age, shall part thee from thy strength, or the brightness of thine eyes shall fail and grow dark; straightway shall it be, princely one, that death shall overcome thee.

"Half a hundred years beneath the clouds I so ruled the Ring-Danes and warded them in war with spear and sword from many a people through this mid-earth, that I counted myself without a foe 'neath the stretch of the heaven. Behold! a change came to my land, grief after joy, when Grendel, the old-time foe, became my invader; ceaselessly from that troubling I suffered exceeding sorrow of spirit.

Thanks be to God, the Eternal Lord, that I have bided in life so long that I may look with mine eyes on this head, gory from the sword.

"Go now to thy mead-bench, honored warrior; taste of the joy of the feast; treasures full many shall be between us twain, when morn shall come."

The Geat was glad at heart and went therewith to find his place, as the wise one had bidden. Then anew, in fair wise, was the feast spread for them, mighty in valor, sitting in the hall. The helm of night darkened down dusky over the bandsmen. The press of warriors all arose; the white-haired prince, the old Scylding desired to seek his bed. The Geat, the valiant shield-warrior, listed well, past the telling, to rest him. Soon the hall-thane, who took care with courteous observance for the hero's every need, such as in that day seafarers should have, led him forth, come from afar, worn with his venture. Then the great-hearted one took his rest.

The hall lifted itself broad and brave with gold. The guest slept within till the black raven, blithe of heart, heralded the joy of heaven. Then the bright sun came gliding over the plain. The warsmen hasted, the athelings were eager to fare again to their people. He who had come to them, the large of heart, would take ship far thence. The brave one bade the son of Ecglaf bear off Hrunting, bade him take his sword, his beloved blade, spake him thanks for its lending, said he accounted it a good war-friend, of might in battle, belied not in words the sword's edge. That was a man great of soul! And when the warriors were in forwardness for the journey, with their gear made ready, the atheling dear to the Danes, the hero brave in the fight, went to the high-seat, where the other was, and greeted Hrothgar.

26

Beowulf spake, the son of Ecgtheow: "We, seafaring ones, come from afar, wish now to say that we mean now to make our way to Hygelac. We have been well entreated here in all man could wish; thou hast dealt well by us. If then on earth, O Lord of Men, I may earn more of thy heart's love by deeds of war than I yet have done, I shall straightway be ready. Should I learn over the stretches of the flood that thy neighbors burden thee with dread, as they that hate thee at times have done, I shall bring a thousand thanes, warriors, to thine help. I know of Hygelac, Lord of the Geat-folk, the people's herd, that though he be young he will uphold me in word and deed that I may do thee full honor and bear to thine aid the spear's shaft, the stay of his strength, when need of men shall be thine. If, furthermore, Hrethric, son of the king, take service at the court of the Geats, he shall find many friends there; far-off lands are better to seek by him that may trust in himself."

Hrothgar spake to him in answer: "Now hath the wise Lord sent these sayings into thy soul. Never heard I man so young in years counsel more wisely. Thou art strong in might and safe in thought, and wise in thy sayings. I account it likely that if it hap the spear, the fierce battle-sword, sickness, or the steel, taketh away the son of Hrethel, thy prince, the people's herd, and thou hast thy life, that the Sea-Geats will have no man better to choose for king, for treasure-warden of the warriors, if thou art willing to rule the realm of thy kinsfolk. Thy brave spirit liketh me, passing well, ever the more, dear Beowulf. Thou hast so wrought that peace shall be between the Geat-folk and the Spear-Danes, and strife be at rest, the guileful onslaughts they have erstwhile undergone. Whilst I rule this wide realm, treasure shall be in common; greeting shall many a one send another by gifts across the gannet's bath; the ringed ship shall bring over the sea offerings and tokens of love. I know the peoples are fast wrought together both toward foe and toward friend, void of reproach in every wise as the way was of old."

Then, thereto, the son of Healfdene, shield of earls, gave him in the hall twelve treasures, bade him make his way with these gifts safe and sound to his dear people, and come again speedily. The king, then, goodly of birth, Lord of the Scyldings, kissed the best of thanes and clasped him about the neck. The tears of the white-haired king fell; old and wise, two things he might look for, but of these the second more eagerly, that they might yet again see one another, mighty in counsel. The man was so dear to him, that he might not bear the tumult of his heart, for in his breast, fast in the bonds of thought, deep-hidden yearning for the dear warrior burned throughout his blood.

Beowulf, gold-proud warrior, trod thence over the grassy earth, rejoicing in his treasure. The sea-goer awaited her master, as she rode at anchor. Oft then, as they went, was the gift of Hrothgar spoken of with praise. That was a king in all things blameless, till old age, that hath scathed many a man, took from him the joys of might.

27

Then came the press of liegemen, passing brave, to the flood; they bare their ringed mail, their linked battle sarks. The land-warden marked the earls' return, as he did before; he greeted not the strangers with fierce words from the cliff's crest, but rode toward them and said that the Weder-folk, the spoilers in their gleaming mail, were welcome as they fared to their ship. The seaworthy craft, the ring-prowed craft on the sand, was laden then with battle-mail, with the horses and treasure. The mast rose high above the holdings from Hrothgar's hoard. He gave the ship's keeper a sword mounted with gold such that thereafter on the mead-benches he was held the more worthy because of that treasure, that sword handed down from of old.

The hero went him into his ship to cleave the deep water, and left the land of the Danes. Then to the mast was a sea-cloth, a sail, made fast by its rope. The sea wood creaked. The wind over the waves did not turn the ship from her course. The sea-going craft fared on, floated forth foamy-necked over the waves, the framed ship over the sea-currents, till they might see the cliffs of Geatland, the well-known forelands. The keel, urged by the wind, ran up and stood fast on the land. Straightway the harbor-guard was at the beach ready, who, already, for a long time, from the shore had gazed out afar, eager to see the dear ones. He bound the broad-bosomed ship to the sand with anchored cables, that the might of the waves might not carry away the goodly timber.

Then Beowulf bade bear up the wealth of princes, the trappings and the plates of gold. It was not far thence for them to go to find Hygelac, the son of Hrethel, where he dwelleth in his homestead, he with his comrades near the sea-wall. The house was passing good, its king in the high hall truly princely, and Hygd, daughter of Hæreth, very young in years, wise, and well-thriven, though she had lived years but few within the city gates. Not close-minded was she, none the less, or too chary in giving of gifts, of treasure-holdings, to the Geat-folk.

Thrytho,[1] dread queen of the people, brought with her fierceness

---

[1]Introduced as a contrast to Hygelac. Jealous pride and haughtiness, leading to morbid suspicions, with a cruel temper, caused her to order the death of certain of her father's (or husband's) followers, till (as another or further story tells) a happy marriage (possibly her second) wrought a change in her.

of soul and dire evil-doing. None so brave of the dear comrades, save her lord, durst undertake to look upon her with his eyes by day, save he might count on bonds of death made ready for him, twisted by the hand; quickly forthwith after his seizing was the sword resolved on, that the deadly blade might shew it forth, make clear his murderous end. That is not a queenly practice for a woman to use, matchless though she be, that a weaver of peace should take away the life of a dear warrior on charge of misdoing. Hemming's kinsman speedily put an end to this. Men, as they drank the ale, told further, that she wrought less of destruction among the people and vengeful onslaughts, so soon as she was given, decked with gold, to the young warrior of proud birth, when she, by her father's behest, sought, journeying over the fallow flood, the hall of Offa, where, henceforward through life, she took exceeding joy in the life fate gave her on the throne, renowned for her goodness, cherished a great love for the prince of men, best, as I have heard tell, between the seas, of all mankind, the race widespread. Therefore Offa, warrior brave with the spear, was held in honor far and wide for his gifts and his deeds in battle. With wisdom he ruled his realm; and of him was Eomo, kinsman of Hemming, grandson of Garmund, mighty in battle, born to be of help to warriors.

28-30[1]

Then went the strong one over the sands, himself with his fellowship, treading the sea-beach, the wide shores. The sun, the candle of the world, shone forth hastening from the south. They pushed on their way, went forward stoutly, to where they heard that the shield of earls, the slayer of Ongentheow, the good king, was parting rings in the city. Beowulf's return was made known speedily to Hygelac, that the safeguard of warriors, his shield-comrade, had come there, still living, to the palace, hale of body from the battle-play to the court. Quickly, as the king bade, was the hall set in readiness within for the way-faring guests.

Then he that had come forth from the strife sat beside the prince

---

[1]The 29th and 30th divisions are not marked. A capital letter appears at line 2039, where there is apparently no break

himself, kinsman beside kinsman, after that his liege lord had greeted
the true man in courteous wise with heartfelt words. The daughter
of Hæreth went through the hall for the mead-serving; she loved the
people, bare the wine-cup to the hands of the Geats. Hygelac began
to question his comrades in fair wise in the high hall; eagerness fret-
ted him to know what the adventures of the Sea-Geats had been:
"How befell it thee in thy faring, dear Beowulf, when thou hadst sud-
den thought to seek battle afar, strife in Heorot, over the salt sea? But
didst thou better in any measure the woe far-rumored of the famed
prince Hrothgar? I brooded because of it in grief of heart with surg-
ing sorrow, nor might I believe in this venture of my dear follower.
Long time I prayed thee not to address the deadly foe, but let the
Spear-Danes themselves come to war with Grendel. Thanks I utter to
God, that I may see thee safe."

Beowulf spake, the son of Ecgtheow: "Known of many men, Lord
Hygelac, is the far-famed meeting, what passage of warfare there
was between Grendel and me, in the place where he wrought the
Victor. Scyldings sorrow far too much. I avenged it all so that none of
Grendel's kin that longest shall live of his loathly race, begirt by the
fenland, need boast of that twilight-outcry.

"I first there betook me to greet Hrothgar in the ring-hall. Soon,
when he knew my purpose, the mighty son of Healfdene awarded
me a seat with his own son. Joyous was the company; never saw I
my life long 'neath the hollow of heaven greater joy among those sit-
ting at mead in hall. Whiles, the great queen, peace bringer between
peoples, went through all the hall, heartened the youths, and often
bestowed a circlet on a warrior, ere she went to her seat. Whiles, the
daughter of Hrothgar bare the ale-beaker before, the press of warriors
to the earls in turn; Freawaru I heard them name her that sat in the
hall, when she gave the embossed treasure-cup to the warriors. She
hath been plighted, young and decked with gold, to the gracious son
of Froda. It hath seemed to the Scyldings' friend, the keeper of the
realm, and he counteth the counsel good, that he through this maid
may set at rest a deal of death-feuds and strifes. Oft and again have
they given troth-pledges after the fall of that people; for a short space
only will the death-spear be lowered, though the bride be goodly.[1]

---

[1]Kluge's interpretation; the passage might also read "after the prince's fall," pos-
sibly with reference to the death of Froda, Ingeld's father, in battle with the
Danes. The whole passage offers difficulty. A current reading, dependent upon a

"Therefore it may ill please[1] the prince of the Heathobards and every thane of the people, when he goeth with his bride into the hall, that his warrior-hosts should do guest's service for a princeling of the Dane-folk; on him gleam forth bequests of their ancient ones, hard and ring-decked, the Heathobards' own, so long as they might wield their weapons, till that they led away to an evil end their dear comrades and their own lives in the sword-play. Then, as he seeth the treasure, there speaketh out at the beer-drinking an old spearsman that keepeth it in mind all of it, how their men were slain by the spear—his heart is fierce within him. In grief of heart he beginneth to try the temper of the young warriors, through the thought of their breasts, and to waken war-havoc, so speaketh this word: 'Canst thou, my friend, recall the sword, the blade beloved, thy father beneath his battle-mask bare to the fight on his last foray when the Danes slew him, where, after the warriors' fall, when hope of requital failed us, the bold Scyldings held the field of slaughter? Now, from among those murderers, some youth or other goeth his way into the hall, making a show of his trappings, vaunteth of that murder, and weareth the treasures thou shouldest rightly have rule of.'

"Thus every moment he spurreth and remindeth with wounding words, till time cometh that the bride's thane, paying debt of life for his father's deeds, sleepeth in his blood through the sword's bite. The other fleeth him thence with his life; he knoweth the land full well. On both sides then the oath-taking of the earls is broken, and there-

---

different emendation, runs, "Often and not seldom, in any place, after a prince's fall, is the death-spear lowered, though the bride be goodly," a gnomic statement followed by Beowulf's forecast of the issue in this special case. Kluge's reading offers less difficulty. After the overthrow of the Heathobards, peace has been preserved only by continual renewal of the treaty between the two peoples, and the marriage will assure its continuance but for a short time.

[1]The poet here endows Beowulf with prophetic foresight in order to introduce into the poem the story of the results of Freawaru's marriage to Ingeld, which were known, no doubt, in a separate story. In place of bringing to an end the feud between the Danes and the Heathobards, the marriage must lead to a renewal of strife, owing to the anger of the Heathobards at seeing one of the bride's retainers decked in armor won in the fight from one of their number. This retainer is killed by the son of the man whose sword he wears, and the feud starts afresh. From a reference in "Widsith," it seems clear that Ingeld later sought out Hrothgar at Heorot, and there received a crushing defeat at the hands of Hrothgar and his nephew Hrothulf. Possibly it was at this time that Heorot was burned; see p. 95 ("Warring surges," etc.) and footnote [2].

after a deadly hatred welleth up in Ingeld, and his love for his wife groweth cooler through the surgings of his sorrow. I deem not therefore the good-will of the Heathobards towards the Danes, or their part in the peace, free from peril of faithlessness, or their friendship a lasting one.

"I must go on, O ring-giver, to speak once more of Grendel, that thou mayest know in full what outcome there was thereafter of the strife, hand to hand, of warriors. When the jewel of heaven had glided away o'er the plains, the stranger-one, the grisly night-foe, came in his wrath to seek us out where we watched, well and strong, o'er the hall. There was a deadly strife and life-ending there for the fated Hondscio; he fell first, the girded warrior; him, famed thane of our kindred, Grendel slew with his teeth, swallowed down wholly the corse of the man we loved. Never the sooner for that was the bloody-fanged slayer, with havoc in heart, minded to go forth again empty-handed from the treasure-hall, but, fierce in his might, me he tried and gripped me with his ready claw. His glove hung,[1] wide and wondrous, made fast with shrewd fastenings; it was all made in skilful wise with devils' wiles and of dragons' skin. His thought was, bold doer of evil, to put me therein, all blameless, and many a one beside; he might not so, when I stood upright in my wrath. Too long is it to tell how I paid the spoiler of the people his dues for each of his evils. There did I, my lord, do honor to thy people by my deeds. He fled away, had part for a while in the joys of life, though his hand kept his track in Heorot, and thence in abjectness, anguished in spirit, fell to the mere-bottom.

"For that deadly strife the friend of the Scyldings (when morning came and we had sat us to the feast) made me bounteous requital with plates of gold and many a treasure. There was song and mirthmaking. The hoary Scylding, after questioning me oft, told of far-off days; whiles, the battle-famed prince woke the harp's joy, the pleasurewood; whiles, he framed a lay true and sorrowful; whiles, the greathearted king told in fitting wise some wondrous story; or at times again the white-haired warrior, in the bondage of age, began to mourn his youth and strength in battle; his heart swelled within him

[1]The word "glove" has been explained as a bag for Grendel's spoils. It has also been used as evidence that the original of Grendel was a bear (compare also the description of his claws; see p. 112), the glove representing what was originally his paw or pad.

when he, in years so old, took thought of their number. Thus the day long we took our pleasure, till another night came to the children of men. Soon then thereafter was Grendel's mother ready to wreak vengeance for her hurt, fared forth in her sorrow; death, and the war-hate of the Weders, had taken away her son. The grisly wife avenged her child; in her might she killed a man—life went forth there from Æschere, the old councillor. Nor might the Dane-folk with fire burn him, death-weary, when morning came, nor lift on the pyre him they loved; she bare off the corse in her fiendish clasp down under the mountain stream. That was the sorest of the sorrows that long had beset Hrothgar, leader of his people. The prince, in grief of soul, adjured me then by thy life to achieve earlship in the moil of the waters, to risk my life and to win renown; he vowed me my meed for it. Then, as is known far and wide, I sought out the grim and grisly warden of the flood's depth. Hand there was locked in hand for a space. The flood welled with blood, and in that hall in the deeps with a matchless blade I hewed off the head of Grendel's mother. Not easily bare I my life away—not yet was I marked for death—but thereafter the shield of earls, the son of Healfdene, bestowed on me many a treasure."

31

"Even thus lived the people's king in due regard of right; in no wise did I lose my just due, the meed of my might, for he gave me treasures, did the son of Healfdene, even such as I myself might wish. These I desire to bring and to tender them thee with joy, O king of men. Still hath every good thing its beginning with thee; save thee I have few close kinsmen, O Hygelac."

He bade them bring in the head-crest in shape of a boar, the helmet high uplifted in battle, the gray burnie, the war-sword won-drously wrought, and his tale framed after: "To me the wise prince Hrothgar gave this battle-gear, laid on me this one behest that first of all I should tell thee his friendship. He said that king Heorogar had it long, the prince of the Scyldings, yet this breast-mail he would not give to his own son, the brave Heoroweard, dear though he was to him. Have thy full joy of it all."

I heard that four horses, apple-fallow, wholly alike, went the same way as the trappings; honor he showed to Hygelac with horses and treasures. So must a kinsman do and not weave a net of cunning for the other, or with hidden craft devise the death of his close comrade. Faithful indeed was his nephew to Hygelac, the strong in battle, and each was mindful for the other's weal.

I heard that he gave to Hygd the collar, the wondrous treasure, marvellously wrought, that Wealhtheow, a king's daughter, gave him, and three horses also, trim of build and shining beneath the saddle. From that time, after the gift of the collar, was her breast well bedecked.

In such wise the warrior renowned, the son of Ecgtheow, bare him bravely through worthy deeds, lived lawfully, slew not at all, when drunken, his hearth-companions. Not ruthless was he of soul, but, bold in strife, kept ward with his utmost might of the generous gift that God had given him. Long had he been scorned, so that the children of the Geats held him unworthy, nor would the lord of the battle-hosts pay him much regard on the mead-bench. They thought surely he was slack, a laggard atheling. There came a change for him, well thriven in honors, from every despite.

Then the shield of earls, the king stout in battle, bade fetch in Hrethel's sword, mounted in gold; there was not then among the Geats a better treasure in the like of a sword. He laid it on Beowulf's lap, and gave him seven thousand pieces, a hall, and a prince's high-seat. Both alike had land by birth-fee in the people's holding, a home, and an ancestral right; to the other beside was the broad kingdom, and in that was the better man.

That he attained afterward, in days to come, through shocks of battle, after Hygelac fell[1] and the war-swords had slain Heardred beneath his shield's shelter, then when the War-Scylfings, stout warriors, sought him out among his victor-folk and overthrew the nephew of Hereric in war; thereafter was it the broad realm fell into the hand of Beowulf.

He ruled it well for fifty years—old then was the king, warden of the land from long past till that a dragon began to be masterful on dark nights, that on the high heath kept watch of a hoard in a lofty stone barrow. Below lay a path not known to men. Therein went some man or other, laid hold eagerly on the heathen hoard, took with his

---

[1] In his foray against the Frisians, Heardred was killed by the Swedes; see footnote [2], p. 143.

band a cup gleaming with gold; he gave it not back though its keeper had been defrauded, as he slept, with thievish craft. The people, the dwellers in the towns, learned how that he was angered thereby.[1]

32

Not with intent and of his own will did this thane of some one of the sons of men, that did him this grievous injury, seek out the mighty dragon-hoard, but because of sore stress, in need of shelter, a man driven by guilt, he fled from blows of anger and betook himself therein. Soon it befell that hideous terror came upon the stranger in that dwelling, yet the wretched one, even as the horror seized him, caught sight of the treasure-cup.[2]

There were many such olden treasures in the earth-house, just as some man, taking heedful care of the mighty heritage of his high kindred, had hid them there, his dear treasures, in days gone by. Death had taken his kinsfolk all away at an earlier time, and the one that of the warrior-host of that people still then longest held on his way, went sorrowing for his friends, yet trusted for such length of years that he might enjoy for a little while that wealth long-treasured. A barrow stood fully ready nigh the sea-waves on the moor, newly made on the foreland, closed fast by sure devices. The guardian of the rings bare within it there the lordly treasure, the heap hard to carry of plate-gold, and spake in few words: "Hold thou now, O earth, now that warriors may not, this wealth of earls. Behold, in thee at the first did good men find it. Death in battle, dread evil, hath taken off every man of my people that hath left this life; they had looked on the joys of the mead-hall. None have I that may wield sword, or burnish the gold-decked vessel or the drinking-cup of price; the warrior host is gone elsewhither. The hard helmet, bedight with its gold, must be spoiled of its platings; they sleep that burnished it, whose

---

[1]The translation of this almost illegible passage is based upon the reconstruction of Bugge and others, as given in Holder's edition.

[2]A passage still more illegible than that above, a line and a half having disappeared beyond recovery. In the translation, the liberty is taken of bridging this gap, but without the introduction of words not in the original.

part it was to make ready the masks of war. And the battle-gear like-wise, that withstood in strife, midst the crash of shields, the bite of the steel, shall crumble with the warrior. The ring-meshed burnie no longer may fare far with the war-prince at the warrior's side. Joy of the harp is not, or delight of the glee-wood; the good hawk swingeth not through the hall, nor doth the swift steed paw the court of the stronghold. Death that despoileth hath sent forth many a one of liv-ing kind." Thus, sorrowful of heart, he made lament with grieving, he, left solitary, for them all wept, reft of gladness, till the flood of death laid hold on his heart.

The old twilight-spoiler, the evil naked dragon, that flaming seeketh out the barrows and flieth by night enfolded in fire, found the joy-giving hoard standing open. Him the earth-dwellers dread exceedingly. He must needs seek out a hoard in the earth, where, old in years, he watcheth the heathen gold; no whit is he the better for it.

Thus three hundred years the spoiler of the people held in the earth a treasure-house, mighty in strength, till that a certain man made him wrathful of heart, bare away a cup of gold to his prince, prayed his lord for a bond of peace. Thus was the hoard despoiled, some part of the ring-treasure carried away, and his boon granted to the man in his need. His lord looked for the first time on that work of men of far-off days.

When the dragon awoke, strife was newly kindled. He snuffed along the rock and, stout of heart, came on the foot-tracks of his foe; in his furtive craft the man had gone too far, too near the drag-on's head. So may one not marked for death, whom the grace of the Wielder stayeth, come forth full readily from his woes and the path of exile. The treasure-warden sought eagerly along the ground, and would fain find the man that had brought this harm on him in his sleep. Hot and savage of heart, he went often all about the mound without, but no man was there in that waste place. Yet had he joy in the coming of battle and the toils of war. Whiles, he went into the mound and sought the treasure-cup; soon knew he for sure some man had found out his gold and his noble treasure. Scarce waited the treasure-keeper till evening came; angered was he then, the barrow-warden; the loathly one was of mind to take payment with fire for his precious cup. Then was the day gone, as the dragon desired. No longer would he bide within wall, but fared forth with flaming, girt with fire. A fearful thing was the feud's beginning for the people of the land, even as it was ended speedily in the hurt that befell their treasure-giver.

33

Then the stranger-one began to spew forth gledes and burn the bright homesteads; the glare of the burning struck terror into men; the loathly flyer through the air was minded to leave naught there alive. The dragon's might was seen far and wide, the fell intent of the instant foe near and far, how the war-spoiler hated and brought low the Geat-folk. He shot back, ere daybreak, to his hoard, to his lordly hall hidden from finding. The dwellers in the land he had beset with flame, with fire and burning. He trusted to his harrow, his war-craft and wall: the hope deceived him.

Speedily then was the terror of it made known to Beowulf for truth, in that his own homestead, fairest of houses, the gift-seat of the Geats, had been consumed in the surging flame. Grief of heart it was to the good king, the greatest of sorrows. The wise man deemed that he had angered bitterly the Ruler, the Eternal Lord, against the ancient law. His breast swelled within him with dark thoughts as was not the way with him.

The fire-drake with his flames had laid in ashes the stronghold, the people's fastness, on its island without. Therefore the war-king, prince of the Geats, planned vengeance upon him. The safeguard of warriors, lord of earls, bade be made for him a battle-shield of marvellous kind, all of iron; he knew readily wood of the forest might not help him, linden-wood against flame. The atheling passing worthy must needs abide the close of his life in the world, and the dragon with him, though he had kept for long his wealth of treasure.

The lord of rings scorned then to seek the far-flier with a host, a large army; he dreaded not the strife for himself, nor made he much of the dragon's skill in battle, of his strength and might, because that erstwhile, hazarding peril, he had come through many an onset, brunt of battle, after he, a hero rich in victory, had cleansed Hrothgar's hall, and in strife grappled Grendel's kinsfellow of that loathly race.

That was not the least of close encounters, in which they slew Hygelac, son of Hrethel, when in Friesland, in storm of battle, the king of the Geats, gracious lord of his people, died of the sword-drink, struck down by the war-blade. Beowulf came thence[1] by his own might; he made use of his swimming. He had, he alone, thirty suits of armor when he went to the sea. In no wise needed the Hetwaras, who had borne out their shields against him, be boastful of their warcraft, for few came away afterward from the mighty hero to seek their homes.

The son of Ecgtheow, hapless and lonely, swam back, at that time, over the stretches of the sea to his people again. There Hygd proffered him the treasure and the kingdom, the rings, and the king's seat; she trusted not her son that he would know how to hold his ancestral seats against stranger folk, seeing Hygelac was dead. Yet not for all that might they in their need in any wise prevail upon the atheling to be Heardred's lord or take on himself the kingdom, but he upheld him among the people with friendly counsel, and in kindly wise through the regard he showed him, till that he came of age and ruled the Weder-Geats. Outlawed men sought him[2] from overseas, the sons of Ohthere; they had rebelled against the helm of the Scylfings, a prince renowned, the best of the sea-kings that gave out treasure in the Swedish realm. Of that came Heardred's end. The hapless son of Hygelac came by his death-wound through the stroke of the sword, and the son of Ongentheow went him back to seek his home, when Heardred lay dead, and let Beowulf hold the king's seat and rule the Geats. He was a good king!

34

In after days he took thought of requital for the downfall of his lord; he was a friend to the hapless Eadgils, aided him across the broad sea with his host, his war-craft and weapons, when in after time the son

---

[1]Hygelac's historic foray is here referred to.

[2]Wyatt's explanation of this somewhat obscure story is the simplest and most plausible. The sons of Ohthere, Eanmund and Eadgils, banished from Sweden for rebellion, take refuge with Heardred. Eanmund is killed in a quarrel by Weohstan (see p. 148 and footnote [1], p. 148). Their uncle, King Onela, son of Ongentheow, in wrath at their harboring with his hereditary foes, invades Geatland, Heardred is slain, and Beowulf succeeds to the throne. Beowulf later aids Eadgils in an invasion of Sweden, when the latter slays Onela on the ice of Lake Wener, as described in the Norse version of the story.

of Ohthere took vengeance on Onela for his chill paths of sorrow, and robbed the king of his life. Thus the son of Ecgtheow had come safe from each strife, each hazardous battle and deed of prowess, till this one day that he must do battle against the dragon.

One of twelve, the lord of the Geats, angered exceedingly, went to look on the fire-drake. He had learned in what wise the feud toward men, the deadly strife, had arisen. The wondrous treasure-cup had come to his lap through the hand of the finder. He that had brought about the strife's beginning was the thirteenth man in the company; held captive, sorrowful at heart, he must needs go thence with them to point out the place. Against his will he went where he knew that earth-hall to be, a burial-place beneath the ground, nigh the surge of the sea and the moil of the waters, that within was full of jewels and woven gold-work. Its fearful guardian, a ready wager of war, had held from of old his golden treasure beneath the earth. It was no easy bargain for any man to go in there.

Then the king, stout in strife, the gold-friend of the Geats, sat him on the foreland, whilst he bade his hearth-comrades farewell. His spirit was sad, flickering, within him and ready for death. Wyrd was very near, that must assail the old man, seek out the treasure of his soul, part asunder life from body. Not long, then, was the life of the atheling enclosed in flesh.

Beowulf spake, the son of Ecgtheow: "In my youth I came safe from many a shock of battle and time of strife: I mind me of all. I was seven years old when the prince of treasure, the gracious lord of his people, King Hrethel, took me at my father's hands, held me and had me, gave me treasure and nurture, mindful of our kinship. I was no whit less loved by him during life as his man in hall than any of his sons, Herebeald and Hæthcyn, or mine own Hygelac. In unfitting wise was the death-bed strewn for the eldest of them by a kinsman's deeds, when Hæthcyn struck him down, his dear lord, with an arrow from his bow of horn; the mark he missed and shot his kinsman, one brother another with a bloody shaft. That was an onslaught gold might not atone for, done of evil design, harrowing to the heart. Be that as it may, the atheling must lose his life unavenged. So also is it sorrowful for an old man to live to see his young son ride upon the gallows-tree; then he gives voice to his grief in words, his song of sorrow, when his son hangeth for a joy to the ravens, and he may not help him, do aught for him, old and burdened with years. Ever is he reminded each morn of his son's going hence; nor hath he wish to await another heir in his house, since one hath by dint of death learned the lesson of his deeds. Overborne by sorrow, he seeth in his son's house the wine-hall left wasted, a resting-place for winds, bereft of its joy; horseman and warrior sleep in the grave; sound of harp is not, nor joy in its courts as once there was.

35

"Then he goeth to his sleeping-place, and, lonely, singeth there his song of sorrow for the one he hath lost; all he hath, his lands and his dwelling-place, hath seemed too large for him alone.

"So, likewise, the helm of the Weders bare a heart swelling with sorrow for Herebeald; he might no whit avenge the feud on the slayer, nor yet spend his hate in deeds of enmity on the warrior, though he was not dear to him. Then, for the grief his heart caused him, he gave up the joys of men and chose the light of God; when he went from life, he left to his sons, as one doth that hath wealth, his land and folk-cities. Then was there hatred and strife betwixt the Swedes and the Geats, warfare over the wide water and fierce clash of war-hosts, after Hrethel died, till that the sons of Ongentheow[1] were forward and keen in the struggle, would not keep peace overseas, but oft made forays in direful wise about Hreosnabeorh. This feud and these deeds of evil my kinsfolk avenged, as was known of all, though another paid for it with his life, a hard bargain; it was a fatal war for Hæthcyn, king of the Geats. Then in the morning, as I heard tell, one brother took vengeance on the other's slayer, when Ongentheow met Eofor. The war-helmet split apart; the old Scylfing

---

[1]Onela and Ohthere made forays into Geatland, and the Geats retaliated, carrying off Ongentheow's queen (compare the later account, p. 155 ff.). Ongentheow in turn invaded Geatland, killed Hæthcyn and recovered his wife. The Geatish army was encompassed, but Hygelac (Hæthcyn's younger brother, the king served and loved by Beowulf) came to the rescue. Ongentheow was driven back to his fastness and there slain (see the fuller account on p. 155 ff.) by Eofor, after he had struck down Eofor's brother, Wolf. These events precede those described, p. 143 and footnote [2], p. 143.

fell livid beneath the stroke; Eofor's hand kept mind of feuds enough, it held not back from the death-blow. I then, in that strife, as it was given me to do, repaid Hygelac with my gleaming sword for the treas- ures he had bestowed on me; he gave over to me land, a homestead, and the joy of its holding. He had no need to be forced to seek from the Gifths, or the Spear-Danes, or in the Swedish lands, a worse war- rior, and buy him for a price. Ever would I be in advance in his host, alone at the front, and so shall I, while life last, make fight, so long as the sword endureth, that oft early and late hath served me, ever since I, before the warrior-hosts, with my hand slew Dæghrefn,[1] fore- fighter of the Hugas. In no wise might he bring trappings and breast- deckings to the Frisian king, but fell, the keeper of the standard, the atheling in his might, in our encounter. The sword's edge was not his slayer, but the battle-grip brake his ribs and his heart's beating. Now must the blade's edge, the hand, and the stout sword, wage war for the treasure."

Beowulf spake, gave forth word of vaunting for the last time: "In my youth I came safe from many a battle; yet, if the fell spoiler seek me out from his earth-hall, will I, the old warden of my people, seek the strife, do deeds worthy of praise."

He greeted then for the last time each of his men, he, the bold helmet-bearer, his dear comrades: "I would bear no sword or other weapon against the dragon, even as I once did with Grendel, wist I how I might else make good my vaunt against the monster. But I may look for hot battle-fire there, for reek and for poison; for this cause I have upon me shield and burnie. Not a foot's length will I give back from the keeper of the barrow, but it shall befall us in fight at the wall, as Wyrd, the ruler of all men, may grant. I am keen of heart so that I forego boasting against the flying foe. Await ye, ye men in your war-gear, clad in your burnies, whether of us twain may fare the better of our wounds after our fight to the death. It is no venture for you, nor is it meet for any man to use his strength against the mon- ster, achieve earlship, save for me alone. By my might shall I gain the gold, or battle, life's peril, shall take your lord."

Then the brave warrior, strong beneath his helmet, rose with his shield, bore his battle-sark beneath the stony steeps, trusted in the strength of a single man; such is not the way of a coward. He that,

---

[1]During Hygelac's foray.

goodly in manly virtue, had come forth from full many a strife and shock of battle, when the foot-bands meet, beheld by the wall an arch of stone standing and a stream breaking out thence from the barrow. The stream's flood was hot with battle-fires; the hero might not endure anywhile, without burning, the stretch below, nigh the hoard, because of the dragon's fire.

Then the prince of the Weder-Geats, for that he was angered, let a word go forth from his breast. The strong of heart stormed; his voice came sounding in, battle clear, under the hoar stone. Hate was roused; the treasure-warden was ware of the hero's speech; there was no more time to seek for peace.

First there came forth from the stone the breath of the monster, the hot fuming of battle. The earth resounded. The warrior beneath the barrow, the lord of the Geats, swung round his battle-shield against the grisly foe. Then was the heart of the coiling one made eager to seek the strife. The good war-king had ere then drawn his sword, handed down from of old, not slow of edge. Terror came to those plotters of harm, each of the other. The ruler o'er friends stood, steadfast of heart, against his broad shield whilst the dragon coiled quickly; in his war gear he waited.

Then came moving on the fiery one, bowed together, hastening to his fate. Inasmuch as Wyrd had not dealt the great king triumph in the strife, his shield guarded well life and body less long than his desire to be let conquer at that time there in the day's prime had looked for. The Lord of the Geats lifted up his hand and struck the fell foe with his mighty sword, so the shining edge weakened on the bone, bit with less might than the folk king, encompassed with evils, had need of. Savage of heart then was the warden of the barrow because of the battle-stroke, and cast forth deadly fire; the fierce flamings of it sprang far and wide. The friend of the Geats was not to boast a far-famed victory. His naked war-sword, his blade passing good, had weakened in the strife as it ought not. No easy journey was it for the son of Ecgtheow to leave the earth-plain; unwilling he must make his home in a dwelling-place elsewhere, for so must every man lay aside the days that pass from him.

It was not long before the fighters met together once more. The keeper of the hoard took heart; his breast rose once again with his breathing. The prince, he that erstwhile had ruled his people, suffered straits, hemmed in by the flames. Not at all did his own close

comrades, sons of athelings, stand about him in press, showing cour-
age in battle, but betook them to the woods to save their lives. The
soul of but one of them swelled with sorrow; naught can ever set
aside kinship in sight of him that judgeth aright.

36

Wiglaf was he named, the son of Weohstan, prince of the Scylfings,
kinsman of Ælfhere, a loved shield-warrior. He saw his lord beneath
the battle-mask laboring from the heat. He bethought him then of
all the honors the prince had in former days bestowed upon him,
the wealthy homestead of the Wægmundings and every folkright his
father owned. He might not then hold back, grasped his shield, the
yellow linden, with his hand, and drew his old sword. That sword was
left among men by Eanmund, son of Ohthere, whom, as a friendless
exile, Weohstan slew[1] in the strife with the edge of his war brand, and
bare to his kinsman his shining helm, his ring-knit burnie, the old
sword of eotens Onela had given him, war-weeds of a comrade, his
battle-gear ready for foray. Weohstan spake not of the feud, though
he had felled the son of the brother of Onela. He kept the trappings
many a year, the sword and burnie, till his son Wiglaf might achieve
earlship as his father had erstwhile done. He gave then to Wiglaf
among the Geats every sort of battle-gear in countless number, and
went forth, being old, on his way hence.

  That was the first time the young warrior had need to take part
with his dear lord in the storm of battle. His soul melted not away,
nor did the sword bequeathed by his kinsman weaken in the strife;
this the dragon learned when they met together.

  Wiglaf spake many a righteous word, for his spirit was sorrowful,
and said to his comrades: "I mind me, the time we drank the mead, we
vowed then to our lord in the beer-hall, who gave us these rings, that
we would requite him for our war-gear, the helmets and swords of
temper, if this-like need should befall him. He chose us for this ven-

---

[1]Shame at killing a friendless exile and guest prevented Weohstan from boast-
ing of his exploit, though the slain man was the nephew of Onela, the hated
foe of the Geats.

ture of his own will from his host, roused us to deeds of glory, and gave me these treasures, because he held us to be good wagers of war with the spear, brave wearers of helmet, even though he, our lord, guardian of his people, thought to achieve this deed of might alone, for that he among all men hath wrought the most of feats of prowess and daring deeds.

"Now is the day come that our liege-lord hath need of the might of good warriors. Let us go to him, help our leader in battle, whilst the heat endure, the grim terror of the flame. God knoweth of me I would much liefer the fire should enfold my body with that of my giver of gold. Unmeet it seemeth me we should bear our shields back home save we first fell the might of the foe, and guard the life of the prince of the Weders. I trow well it were not his due, long owed him, that he alone of the flower of the Geats should bear the trouble and sink in the strife. Sword and helm, burnie and shield, shall be one between us."

He went then through the slaughter-reek, bore his helmet to his lord's aid: "Dear Beowulf, do all well, even as thou didst vow afore-time in thy youth, that thou wouldst not, yet living, let thy glory fall away. Now must thou, steadfast atheling, famed for thy deeds, guard thy life with all thy might. I shall aid thee."

After these words the dragon, the foe fell and fearful, came in wrath a second time, bedight with surges of flame, to seek the men, his loathing. The shield of the young spearsman burned to the boss in the waves of fire, and his burnie might yield him no aid. But the young retainer went him speedily under his kinsman's shield, for his own was consumed utterly by the fire. Then once more the war-king bethought him of the meeds of glory, and in the might of his strength struck with his war-sword, so that it drave into the dragon's head, urged by hate. Nægling was broken; the sword of Beowulf, old and gray-hued, betrayed him in the strife; it was not given him that edge of steel might help him in the battle. His hand was too strong, as I have heard tell, trying overmuch any sword by its blow; when he bore to the fight a weapon wondrous hard, no whit was he the better for it.

Then the spoiler of the people, the fell fire-drake, was of mind a third time for the strife, rushed, hot and battle grim, upon the valiant one, when he gave him ground, and with his bitter fangs took in all the throat of the hero. Beowulf was bloodied with his life-blood; the blood welled forth in waves.

37

I heard tell that then in the folk-king's need his earl gave proof of lasting prowess, of the strength and boldness born in him. He heeded not the head of the dragon, albeit the brave man's hand was burned in aiding his kinsman, so he might, the mailed warrior, smite the fell foe a little lower, in such wise the shining sword, decked with gold, sank in, and the fire thereafter began to fail. Then the king came to himself once more, and drew the war-dagger, bitter and sharp for battle, he wore on his burnie. The helm of the Weders cut the dragon in two in the middle. They felled the foe, their prowess cast forth his life, and they both, kinsman athelings, had overthrown him. Such a man should a warrior, a retainer, be in time of need.

That was the last triumphant hour, through his own deed, of the king's work in this world. The wound the earth-dragon before had given him began then to burn and swell. He soon found that a dire evil, poison within, was rising in his breast. The atheling, wise of thought, went him then to sit on a seat by the wall; he looked on the work of giants, how the stone-arches, firm upon their pillars, upheld within the ever-enduring earth-hall. His retainer, worthy beyond telling, laved then with his hands with water the king far-famed, his own dear lord, bloodstained and spent with battle, and loosed his helmet.

Beowulf brake forth in speech, spake despite his hurt, his livid death-wound; he knew well he had had his day's while and the pleasures of earth, that all his tale of days was past now and death ever so near. "Now would I give my war-weeds to my son, had but any heir belonging to my body been given to follow me. I have ruled the people fifty years; no folk-king was there of them that dwelt about me durst touch me with his sword or cow me through terror. I bided at home the hours of destiny, guarded well mine own, sought not feuds with guile, swore not many an oath unjustly. Therefore, though sick now unto death with my wounds, I may have joy of it all, in that the Ruler of Men may not blame me for murder of kinsmen, when life leaveth my body.

"Now go thou quickly, dear Wiglaf, to look on the hoard under the hoar rock, now that the worm lieth slain, sleepeth sore wounded, bereft of his treasure. Be in haste now, so I may see the old wealth-holdings, the treasure of gold, and behold with gladness the bright jewels curiously set; so may I, because of this wealth of treasure, the softlier yield up my life and lordship I have held for long."

38

Then, as I heard tell, the son of Weohstan hearkened quickly after these words the bidding of his wounded lord, sick from the strife, and bore his ring-mesh, his woven battle-sark, under the roof of the barrow. The valorous thane, rejoicing in victory, when he had passed by the seat, saw many a jewel of price, gold glittering strewn on the ground, wondrous things on the wall, and the den of dragon, the old twilight-flier—jars standing, vessels of men of far-off days, with no one to burnish them, stripped of their deckings. Many a helmet was there, old and rusted, and many an arm-ring, woven with shrewd skill. Store of treasure, gold in the earth, may easily make any one of mankind over-proud, let him hide it that will. Likewise he saw a standard all of gold hanging high over the hoard, most wondrous of works, weft by skilled craft. A light came from it, so he might see the floor and look over the treasures. No sign of the dragon was there, for the sword's edge had taken him away.

I heard tell that one man then despoiled the board within the barrow, the ancient handiwork of giants, and filled his bosom as he willed with wine-cups and platters; the standard also, brightest of beacons, he took away. The sword of the old king with its edge of iron had ere then given its hurt to him that long time had been keeper of the treasure and had waged at midnight the fire's terror, flooding forth, in deadly wise, hot before the hoard, till that he died a bloody death.

The messenger was in haste; he was eager to go back, spurred on by the treasures. Desire fretted him, the high-souled youth, to know if he should find the lord of the Weders, so sorely sick, alive still in the place where he had left him. Then, with the treasures, he found the mighty prince, his lord, bleeding, at his life's end. Once more he began to cast water upon him, till the word's point brake through the hidden thought of the breast.

Beowulf spake; the old man in his sorrow looked on the gold:

"For these treasures I here behold I give thanks in words to the Lord
of All, the King of Glory, the Eternal Lord, for that it is given me ere
the day of death to win the like for my people. Now have I trafficked
the laying down of my life, nigh spent, for this hoard of treasure.
Look ye now to my people's needs, I maybe here no longer. Bid the
battle-famed warriors build me a fair mound after the burning on the
sea-headland. It shall lift itself, for a reminder to my people, high on
the Whale's Ness, that seafarers hereafter, that drive their deep ships
afar o'er the mist of the floods, shall call it Beowulf's Barrow."

The brave-hearted prince took from his neck a golden circlet, gave
to his thane, the young spearsman, his gold-decked helm, his ring,
and his burnie, and bade him have his joy of them: "Thou art the
last of the Wægmundings, our kindred; Wyrd hath taken away all my
kinsmen, the earls in their might to their fate. I must after them."

That was the last thought of the old king's heart, ere he made
choice of the pyre, the hot death-surges. His soul went forth from his
bosom to find the award of the steadfast in right.

39

Then it went sorely indeed with the youth to see his dearest one laid
on the earth at his life's end meeting stress so sore. His slayer lay
there likewise, the grisly earth-dragon, bereft of life, overborne by his
spoiling. The dragon with his twisting coils might no longer rule his
treasure-hoards, for the edge of the steel, the hard handiwork of ham-
mers, nicked in battle, had taken him hence, so that the far-flier fell
to the ground, stilled by his wounds, nigh to his treasure-house; in
no wise might he sweep sporting through the air at midnight, make
show of himself, proud of his treasure-holdings, for he fell to earth
through the handiwork of the leader in battle. Truly, as I have heard
tell, it profiteth men but few, through might-possessing and daring in
every deed, for one to make onset against a poison-breathing spoiler,
or lay hand to his treasure-hall, should he find the warden waking
and housed in his barrow. A deal of lordly treasure was paid for by
Beowulf through his death. Each had come to the end of this life that
passeth.

It was not long then that the laggards in war gave up the wood, the traitorous weaklings, ten of them together, that durst not erstwhile make play with their spears in their liege-lord's dire need, but who bare now, with shamed faces, their shields and war-weeds, where the old man lay. They looked on Wiglaf. Wearied he sat, he, the retainer, at his lord's shoulder, and tried to rouse him with water. No whit it availed him; eagerly as he might wish it, he might not keep life in his leader, nor turn one whit the will of the Ruler. God's doom was law in ruling the deeds of every man, as now still it doth.

To the youth then was a grim answer easy to find for those whose courage before that had left them. Wiglaf spake, the son of Weohstan; sorrowful of heart, the hero looked on them he scorned: "This, lo! may he say that hath mind to speak the truth, that the lord ye owned, who gave ye the treasures, the war-gear ye stand in, then, when he on the ale-bench oft bestowed on those sitting in the hall, he the king on his thanes, helmets and burnies such as were the goodliest he might find far or near, that he then, first and last, in wretched wise threw away that battle-gear, so soon as warfare should befall him. Surely not at all had the folk-king need to boast of his comrades in battle—yet God, the Giver of Victory, willed it for him that he all alone, when he had need of prowess, should approve himself with the sword's edge. I was able to give him but little aid in guarding his life in the struggle, and yet, howsoever beyond my power, I did make beginning to help my kinsman. Ever, when I struck the deadly foe with my sword, was he worse for it, and the fire surged less strongly from his head. Defenders too few thronged about the king when the hour came to him. Now shall taking of treasure and gift of swords, every joy you were born to, and right of subsistence, fail from your kindred. Every man of your homesteads shall go void of his land-right, after athelings afar hear tell of your flight, of your infamous deed. Death is better for every earl than a life of dishonor."

40

Then he bade word be given of the battle's toil to the fastness up over the sea-cliff, where the band of earls, sorrowful of heart, had sat holding their shields the day long since morning, looking for one of these two, his last day or the home-coming of the dear warrior. He who rode up the headland was silent touching little of the new tidings, but told them truly in hearing of all: "Now is the lord of the Geats, the bountiful giver of the Weder folk, fast in the bed of death; on the resting-place of slaughter he abideth by the dragon's doing. Beside him lieth the life-queller, sickened by the dagger's thrusts; with his sword he might deal no wound to the monster. Wiglaf, the son of Weohstan, sitteth over Beowulf, one earl beside the other lying lifeless, holdeth head-watch with reverent care for friend and foe.

"Now is a time of war to be looked for by the people when the fall of the king becometh known far and wide to Franks and Frisians.[1] The grievous strife with the Hugas was conceived when Hygelac came faring with a fleet to the Frisians' land, when the Hetware humbled him in battle, speedily attained through greater might, that the armed warrior must bow him to his fall. He fell in the midst of his fighting-bands; he, the leader, gave out no treasure to the warriors. The good-will of the Merovingian[2] hath ever since been withheld from us.

"Nor do I look any whit for peace or good-faith from the Swede-folk,[3] for it was known far and wide that Ongentheow robbed Hæthcyn Hrethling of life nigh Ravens' Wood, when in reckless pride the War-Scylfings first sought the Geat-folk. Soon the old father of Ohthere, ancient and terrible in battle, gave an answering blow, slew the king skilled in sea-craft, set free from captivity his wife, mother of Onela and Ohthere—he the old man, his consort, bereft of her gold—and followed then his deadly foes till they might barely flee away to the Ravens' Wood, their leader lost. Then with an exceeding host he beset those the sword had left, spent with their wounds, oft the night long menaced that forlorn band with woe, said that in the morning he would slay some with the sword's edge, some on the gallows-tree to be a joy to the birds. Comfort came again to them, sorrowful of heart, with the first of the day, so soon as they heard Hygelac's horn and trumpet-call, when the good king came following along their track with the flower of his people."

---

[1]An allusion to Hygelac's foray.
[2]The Merovingian king of the Franks. This reference seems to prove that the poem was composed before the downfall of the Merovingian dynasty in 752.
[3]Another and fuller version of the story told on p. 145; compare also footnote [1], p. 145. The messenger rightly fears the Swedes may seek vengeance, now that Beowulf is dead.

41

"The bloody pathway of Swedes and Geats, the storm of slaughter of the fighters, was plain to see far and wide how the one folk and the other together had spurred on the strife. Ongentheow, goodly warrior, old and much sorrowing, went him then with his comrades to seek his fastness, and turned him toward the heights. He had heard tell of Hygelac's prowess in war, his glorious might in battle, and he trusted not to withstand him, to be able to hold back the sea-men, the ocean-voyagers, or to keep his hoard, his children, and wife; the old man bent him back thence to his wall of earth.

"Chase then was given to the Swede-folk, and their standard to Hygelac; they went forth over the plain of peace,[1] after the Hrethlings thronged tip to the fastness. The white-haired Ongentheow was brought to a halt there by the sword's edge, in such wise the folk-king must yield him to the single will of Eofor. Wrathfully Wulf Wonreding reached for him with his weapon, so that the blood from the blow sprang forth from his veins beneath his hair. Nevertheless the old Scylfing was not dismayed, but repaid forthwith that death stroke with a worse return, after he, the folk-king, had turned toward him, nor might the swift son of Wonred give an answering blow, for the old man had already shorn through the helmet on his head so that he must bow him blood stained, and fall to earth; not as yet was he given over to death, for he grew well again, though the wound had laid hold on him. Then the doughty thane of Hygelac, when his brother was laid low, let his broad blade, the old sword forged by the eotens, break, over across the shield's wall, the giant-huge helmet. Then Ongentheow, the king, the shepherd of his people, bowed him down; he was hurt to the life. There were many then that bound up Eofor's brother, lifted him speedily, when it was granted them to have command of the battlefield, the while the warrior spoiled the other, took from Ongentheow his burnie of iron, hard hilted sword, and helmet therewith, bare to Hygelac the old man's war-gear. He took the trappings and made Eofor fair promise of reward before the people, and likewise fulfilled it. The lord of the Geats, the son of

---

[1]Not clear; sometimes regarded as a proper name. Perhaps the plain before, or the open space within, a "peace-city," or secure fastness of a people, associated with it in name and itself comparatively free from danger of marauding attacks.

Hrethel, when he came to his home, repaid Eofor and Wulf for their stress of battle with exceeding treasure, gave each of them a hundred thousand pieces' worth of land and linked rings, nor durst any man on earth make scorn of the reward, seeing they had wrought deeds of fame with their swords. And further, of his grace, he gave Eofor his only daughter to wed, to be a pride to his home."

"This is the feud and the hatred, the mortal strife between men, by reason of which, as I foresee, because of the fall of their warriors, the Swede-folk, the bold Scylfings, will seek us out, when they hear that our lord is lifeless, he that erstwhile held hoard and realm against them that hate us, acted for his people's good, or, yet more, did deeds of earlship.

"Now it is best as soon as may be that we look upon our folk-king, where he lies, and bring him, that gave us rings, on his way to the pyre. Nor shall a part only consume away with the valiant one, for the hoard of treasure is there, gold uncounted, dearly bought, and even now, at the last, he purchased these rings with his own life; these shall the flame swallow up, the fire hide away, nor forsooth shall an earl wear these treasures for remembrance, nor fair maid have the ring-jewel about her neck, but, sad of heart, reft of her gold, oft and not once alone, shall tread the land of exile, now that the leader in battle has laid aside laughter, revel, and the joys of mirth. Because of this shall many a spear, cold in the dawning, be held in close clasp, lifted up in the hand; the sound of the harp shall in no wise rouse up the warrior, but the dark raven, all alert over the fallen, shall utter his cry over and over, and tell the eagle how well he hath sped at the feasting, the while with the wolf he despoiled the slain." Thus it was the bold warrior told his hateful tidings; he told little enough untrue in his words or forebodings.

The band all arose and went in sorrow, with welling tears, beneath the Eagles' Ness to look on the sight strange to see. They found him who had given them rings in former days making his bed of rest lifeless on the sand. The last day of the good warrior had come in such wise that he, the war-king, the prince of the Weders, had died a death to marvel at. First there they saw the strange wight, the loathly worm, lying on the plain before him. The fire-drake, grim and grisly, was scorched with fire; he was fifty foot-lengths long as he lay. Erstwhile by night he had for his own the joys of the air, and went him down thereafter to seek his den; now he was fast in death and had made last use of his earth-caves. By him stood cups and jars; dishes rested there and costly swords, rusted and eaten through, even as they had lain housed there in the earth's bosom a thousand years. That inheritance exceeding mighty, the gold of men of olden time, had then been placed under a spell, so that no man might lay hand on the ring-hall, unless God Himself, the true King of Victory, Who is man's safeguard, should grant it to him He pleased, even such a man as seemed to Him meet, to open the hoard.

42

Then was it plain to see that he who wrongfully plundered the treasure therein beneath the wall throve not in his venture. Its warden first slew some few of the folk, and then was the feud fulfilled with vengeance in wrathful wise. Matter for wonder is it in what place it shall befall, when an earl, renowned for his prowess, shall reach the end of his life's span, when a man may no longer dwell in the mead-hall with his kinsfolk. So was it with Beowulf when he sought the warden of the barrow and that shrewd encounter; of himself he knew not in what wise his parting from the world would come. The mighty prince who placed the treasure there so laid it under a deep curse till Doomsday, that the man who should spoil that place should be guilty of sin, prisoned in evil places, made fast in hell-bonds, and punished with plagues. The hero was not eager for treasure; rather had he first looked for the grace of the Owner of All.

Wiglaf spake, the son of Weohstan: "Oft must many earls through the act of one man suffer evil, even as hath happened to us. We might not make our dear lord, shepherd of his people, accept aught of good counsel, not to meet the warden of the gold, but to let him lie where he had long been, and abide in his dwelling-place till the world's end. He held to his high destiny. The hoard is ours to see, come to us in woeful wise; too hard was the fate that drew the king thither.

"I was therein and looked upon it all, on the treasures in the hall, seeing it was granted me, though surely not in friendly wise, and a way allowed me in under the earth-wall. With haste I grasped with my hands a great and mighty burden of the hoarded treasure and bare it out hither to my king. He was still alive, aware of what passed and having his understanding. Of full many things spake the old man in his grief, and bade greet you all, and asked that ye build, because of your friend's deeds, on the place where his pyre should stand, a barrow lofty, great and memorable, even as he was of men the warrior worthiest through the wide earth, whilst he might have joy in the wealth of his cities.

"Let us now haste to behold a second time and to search out the heaped-up treasure, curiously fashioned, this marvel that is beneath the wall. I shall guide you so ye may see, nigh at hand, rings and broad gold enough. Let the bier, looked to straightway, be ready when we come forth, and then let us bear our lord, the one we loved, where he must long wait him in the Almighty's keeping."

The son of Weohstan, the warsman bold in battle, gave order that many of the warriors, such as owned dwellings and ruled the folk, be bidden fetch wood for the pile from afar to where the king should be burned: "Now shall the fire, the dark flame as it waxeth, swallow up the strength of warriors, who oft hath breasted the iron shower, when the storm of shafts, sped by the string, shot over the shield-wall, and the arrow, spurred by its feathering, fulfilled its duty, drave home the barb."

Speedily the wise son of Weohstan called together from the king's following seven of the best thanes, and went, as one of eight, beneath the roof of the foe. One of the warriors who went before them bare in his hand a burning light. There was no taking of lots as to who should spoil that hoard after the men had seen any of it resting unguarded and lying at loss in the hall; little did any mourn at bearing thence most speedily the precious treasure. They thrust the dragon also, the worm, over the sea-cliff, let the wave take him, the flood enfold the warden of the treasure. Then was the twisted gold, quite beyond reckoning, loaded upon a wain, and the atheling was borne, the gray battle-prince, to the Whale's Ness.

43

Then the Geat-folk made ready for him a pile, as he had prayed them, firmly based on the earth and hung with helmets and shields and bright burnies; with grief the warriors laid in the midst of it their great prince, their lord beloved. Then began the warriors to quicken on the cliff the greatest of death-fires; the wood-smoke rose dark above the pitchy flame, while the fire roared, blent with the sound of weeping as the turmoil of the wind ebbed, till, hot in the hero's breast, it had crumbled the bone frame. With thoughts left void of gladness and with sorrow of heart, they made their lament for their liege lord's death. His wife, likewise, in deepest grief, her hair close bound, made her song of mourning again and yet again for Beowulf—that she foresaw with grievous dread days of evil for herself, many a death-fall, terror of battle, shame and captivity.[1]

Heaven swallowed up the smoke. Then the Weder-folk built a burial-mound on the cliff that was high and broad, seen afar by the seafarer, and they made it, the beacon of the one who was mighty in battle, in ten days. They carried a wall about the remains of the fire, the goodliest they who were most wise might contrive. In the barrow they placed the rings and jewels, all the trappings likewise which the men of bold heart had taken before from the hoard. They let the earth keep the treasures of earls and the gold lie in the ground where it still now abideth, as useless to men as it was aforetime.

Then about the mound rode the sons of athelings brave in battle, twelve in all. They were minded to speak their sorrow, lament their king, frame sorrow in words and tell of the hero. They praised his earlship and did honor to his prowess as best they knew. It is meet that a man thus praise his liege-lord in words, hold him dear in his heart, when he must forth from the body to become as a thing that is naught.

So the Geat-folk, his hearth-comrades, grieved for their lord, said that he was a king like to none other in the world, of men the mildest and most gracious to men, the most friendly to his people and most eager to win praise.

---

[1]The translation is here based on Bugge's reconstruction of an illegible passage.

AMERICAN LITERATURE

Little Women — Louisa May Alcott
The Last of the Mohicans — James Fenimore Cooper
The Red Badge of Courage and *Maggie* — Stephen Crane
Selected Poems — Emily Dickinson
Narrative of the Life and Other Writings — Frederick Douglass
The Scarlet Letter — Nathaniel Hawthorne
The Call of the Wild and *White Fang* — Jack London
Moby-Dick — Herman Melville
Major Tales and Poems — Edgar Allan Poe
The Jungle — Upton Sinclair
Uncle Tom's Cabin — Harriet Beecher Stowe
Walden and *Civil Disobedience* — Henry David Thoreau
Adventures of Huckleberry Finn — Mark Twain
The Complete Adventures of Tom Sawyer — Mark Twain
Ethan Frome and *Summer* — Edith Wharton
Leaves of Grass — Walt Whitman

WORLD LITERATURE

Tales from the 1001 Nights — Sir Richard Burton
Don Quixote — Miguel de Cervantes
The Divine Comedy — Dante Alighieri
Crime and Punishment — Fyodor Dostoevsky
The Count of Monte Cristo — Alexandre Dumas
The Three Musketeers — Alexandre Dumas
Selected Tales of the Brothers Grimm — Jacob and Wilhelm Grimm
The Iliad — Homer
The Odyssey — Homer
The Hunchback of Notre-Dame — Victor Hugo
Les Misérables — Victor Hugo
The Metamorphosis and *The Trial* — Franz Kafka
The Phantom of the Opera — Gaston Leroux
The Prince — Niccolò Machiavelli
The Art of War — Sun Tzu
The Death of Ivan Ilych and Other Stories — Leo Tolstoy
Around the World in Eighty Days — Jules Verne
Candide and *The Maid of Orléans* — Voltaire
The Bhagavad Gita — Vyasa

BRITISH LITERATURE

Beowulf — Anonymous
Emma — Jane Austen
Persuasion — Jane Austen
Pride and Prejudice — Jane Austen
Sense and Sensibility — Jane Austen
Peter Pan — J. M. Barrie
Jane Eyre — Charlotte Brontë
Wuthering Heights — Emily Brontë
Alice in Wonderland — Lewis Carroll
The Canterbury Tales — Geoffrey Chaucer
Heart of Darkness and Other Tales — Joseph Conrad
Robinson Crusoe — Daniel Defoe
A Christmas Carol and Other Holiday Tales — Charles Dickens
Great Expectations — Charles Dickens
Oliver Twist — Charles Dickens
A Tale of Two Cities — Charles Dickens
The Waste Land and Other Writings — T. S. Eliot
A Passage to India — E. M. Forster
The Jungle Books — Rudyard Kipling
Paradise Lost and *Paradise Regained* — John Milton
The Sonnets and Other Love Poems — William Shakespeare
Three Romantic Tragedies — William Shakespeare
Frankenstein — Mary Shelley
Dr. Jekyll and Mr. Hyde and Other Strange Tales — Robert Louis Stevenson
Kidnapped — Robert Louis Stevenson
Treasure Island — Robert Louis Stevenson
Dracula — Bram Stoker
Gulliver's Travels — Jonathan Swift
The Time Machine and *The War of the Worlds* — H. G. Wells
The Picture of Dorian Gray — Oscar Wilde

ANTHOLOGIES

Four Centuries of Great Love Poems

The text of this book is set in 11 point Goudy Old Style, designed by American printer and typographer Frederic W. Goudy (1865–1947).

The archival-quality, natural paper is composed of recyclable products made from wood grown in sustainable forests; the manufacturing processes conform to the environmental regulations of the country of origin.

The finished volume demonstrates the convergence of Old-World craftsmanship and modern technology that exemplifies books manufactured by Edwards Brothers, Inc.
Established in 1893, the family-owned business is a well-respected leader in book manufacturing, recognized the world over for quality and attention to detail.

In addition, Ann Arbor Media Group's editorial and design services provide full-service book publication to business partners.